CIBI

Simple Japanese-inspired meals
to share with family and friends

Meg and Zenta Tanaka

hardie grant books

CONTENTS

This book uses 15 ml (½ fl oz) tablespoons and 250 ml (8½ fl oz) cup measures.

CIBI: ライフを楽しむために

誰もが昔おちびちゃんだった頃、初めて見て触ったりしたものへの
興味は大きく、自由な発想で工夫をして遊びに使ったりしていたもの
です。好奇心に満ち溢れていたその時の時間と喜びを思い出し、
新鮮な気持ちを常に持っていたい。'CIBI'という名前はそんな想いで
つけられています。

CIBI は、ライフを楽しくするコンセプトストアとして、２００８年にメルボ
ルンにオープン。その後、２０１７年に東京店に２店舗目をオープン
しました。日本の衣食住の考えをもとに、空間、デザイン、食事において
'Head, Hands, Heart（考える、創る、伝える）'をキーワードにお店を
構成しています。

心地よい空間、素敵なデザイン、美味しい食事が集う場所には、人が
あつまり、笑顔が生まれ、小さな幸せが増えていく。それは国境を越え
世界共通で繋がる本質だと、私たちは信じています。CIBI の 'Head,
Hands, Heart' を表現する料理と食の考え方はシンプルです。
「美味しい食べ物は、私たちを幸せにする。」これは、あらゆる事柄に影
響する軸となっている私たちの信条です。

このクックブックは、和の繊細さと西洋の色をミックスさせたCIBI スタ
イルの料理をご紹介するとともに、私たちのフードフィロソフィーが
ぎゅっと詰まった一冊になりました。自分たちのルーツでもある、健康
的で素晴らしい和食の文化を世界のより多くの方々にお伝えしたい、
という想いも込めました。世界中の食卓で、和食材をもっと身近に
楽しんでもらえるきっかけになれたら嬉しいです。

CIBI の考える食事とは、食べ物を食べるという行為だけではなく、
会話を楽しむ機会でもあります。一緒に笑って楽しいひとときを共有
すること。日々の瞬間を鮮やかにするのは、人と人とが共有した時間
そのものかもしれません。生活を豊かにするアイディア、暮らしを彩るプ
ロダクトを、食べることの楽しさや喜びにプラスして。素敵な食事の時
間をどうデザインするか、私たちはいつもワクワクしながら考えています。

この本を読んでくださる世界中の方々が、大切な家族や友人と一緒に、
CIBI スタイルのお料理で美味しく楽しい食事の時間を味わっていただ
けますように。

この本を通じてライフをより楽しんでもらえたら幸いです。

CIBI: IT'S ABOUT ENJOYING LIFE

In Japanese, cibi (pronounced 'chi-bee') means 'a little one'. Each one of us was once a cibi, enjoying that pure and innocent time when we could do whatever we liked. A cibi is always curious, exploring and playing. A cibi treasures their favourite things and relishes favourite foods to satisfy a healthy appetite. Their natural sense of delight means that a cibi always fills a space with warmth.

We opened CIBI, our concept store – a multi-purpose cafe, store, event and neighbourhood space – in 2008 as a way to enrich the everyday lives of our customers, team, suppliers and our neighbourhood. Our core philosophy – *head, hands, heart* – encapsulates who we are and what we do.

With our *heads*, we appreciate the healthy balance and wellness in each serving of food and the form and functionality of each product used in its making. With our *hands*, we engage all of the senses through the physical pleasures of creating and eating. With our *hearts*, we enjoy the colours, tastes and experiences in each mouthful of food and the richness of the space in which we share it.

Head, hands, heart is about showing people how to enjoy life and make each day special by sharing fresh, simple meals with your loved ones. In this book, we invite you to taste our food, experience our space and truly enjoy the small pleasures of a life well lived.

These recipes reflect CIBI's signature style: a blend of traditional Japanese ingredients and cooking methods with western flavours and seasonal produce, creating unique dishes that nourish body and soul. Japanese cooking can seem intimidating, but it doesn't have to be! This book is full of accessible recipes that will introduce you to the many ways you can infuse your cooking with beautiful Japanese flavours to make each day a little bit special. They are simple, yet very satisfying, and made to be shared with friends and family.

At CIBI, our approach to food is simplicity itself. Using the tastiest seasonal ingredients, good produce and a healthy balance of vegetables, fruits, fish and meats, we create a menu of homely dishes to excite the senses and feed the cibi in you. We hope you'll enjoy cooking these recipes at home and that they bring you smiles and happiness.

Eat well, and be healthy and happy.

OUR PHILOSOPHY

CIBI is about much more than food – it is the opportunity to share conversation, laughter, good health and joy. It is both an individual and shared experience that inspires and fills each day with special moments. A good meal and shared community feeds both body and soul.

CIBI is:
the smile we get from our customers in the morning,
the greetings that accompany the delivery of fruit and vegetables,
the sound of steaming milk that makes us feel warm in winter,
the aromas of cooking helping everyone move a little faster,
the magic moment of tasting unexpected flavours and combinations,
the sip of a cool drink from a beautiful handmade glass,
and the delight of discovering something new to you.
It's browsing products and discovering their origin and history,
satisfying your curiosity to make food and products more meaningful,
the sun beaming in, warm and inviting,
the sharing of friendly conversation,
the reminder that simple is very often best.
It's the comfortable space where you always feel good,
and knowing that you can enjoy it each and every day!

AT CIBI, WE LIKE TO COMBINE WHO WE ARE WITH WHERE WE ARE.

When we first created the CIBI concept, we kept turning to the Japanese tenet I-Shoku-Jyu, which we interpret as Beautiful Design, Wholesome Balanced Food and Comfortable Space. Over time, we refined it into something even simpler: *head, hands, heart*. These core values touch every recipe in this book and every step in our cooking process, from selecting ingredients to savouring the very last grain of rice on our plate. They are our common sense guide to staying true to ourselves and the CIBI concept.

Use fresh seasonal produce

When you grow up in the Japanese countryside, eating seasonal ingredients comes naturally – happily, they are usually the best and cheapest ingredients around. Japan experiences four distinct seasons, which means that produce reaches its peak at different times of the year. These changing seasons are reflected in Japanese menus, which feature fresh dishes that meet the body's needs. Refreshing in summer, warming in winter – what a lovely way to get into a healthy rhythm with nature! Every vegetable, fruit and fish has its season: the time when it is plentiful, at peak ripeness and at its health-giving best.

Stay true to the taste of each ingredient

We like to take advantage of the taste of each ingredient. This comes from Meg's upbringing in Japan and from cooking at home – her mum was always busy, but loved to cook and eat good food. We enjoy eating dishes where we can taste and appreciate each ingredient, knowing they were cooked well to preserve what makes them special. When they lose their identity in a dish, it reduces the pleasure of eating it. Treating ingredients well is also linked to health and wellness. If your ingredients are less than fresh or you overcook them, you will lose some of the nutritional value and life-giving benefits unique to each one.

OUR APPROACH TO FOOD IS SIMPLICITY ITSELF.

WE STRIVE TO CREATE
THOUGHTFUL DISHES
WHERE INGREDIENTS
ARE NICELY BALANCED
AND COMPLEMENTARY,
MAKING THEM
NOURISHING FOR
BODY AND SOUL.

Balance the ingredients in each dish

Cooking and eating is all about balance. Simply eating a particular food doesn't make us healthy. Our body doesn't work like a car where you simply add petrol and oil. Rather, it requires a balanced intake to ensure we are physically well and to give us the happiness of true wellbeing. We strive to create thoughtful dishes where ingredients are nicely balanced and complementary, making them nourishing for body and soul.

Take time to savour your food

The Japanese proverb hara-hachi-bun-me means 'eating until you are 80 per cent full is eating in moderation'. If you eat too much, your body becomes unwell. At CIBI, our menu is designed with moderate portion sizes in mind so that you will feel great after finishing a meal rather than stuffed, and you have room to enjoy our petite sweets and coffee or tea. We believe this contributes to good health, provides a great eating experience and reduces waste.

Eat local

At CIBI, we like to combine who we are with where we are, and want the flavour of our meals to reflect this, so we add a Japanese touch to the finest local ingredients and their presentation. Living in Australia for many years has significantly influenced our cooking – it is a big part of who we are, just like the meals we have eaten and experienced in the past. We also cook with traditional Japanese flavours so that our Australian-born children learn about our history and experience their heritage.

Eating is also about presentation

Creating a CIBI moment is not only about food and cooking; it is also about table setting and entertainment. Complete coordination is an important part of CIBI omotenashi (hospitality): it helps create moments you will enjoy and remember.

People often come to CIBI to shop and find beautiful artisan products for their home or friends as a gift. We cherish the moment we help someone find that special gift that will prompt a smile in the recipient. In our design store, we sell select products from all around Japan, chosen to inspire and give our lives extra pleasure. Each product has a meaning and purpose that we hope people will simply enjoy, on special occasions and in everyday life.

In Japan, presentation is an art. From hearty winter one-pot dishes through to elaborate Oshou-gatsu (New Year) feasts, how each dish is served – and what it is served on – reflects local arts, crafts and manufacture. The tableware and table decorations reflect the seasons and the occasion.

Events that spark inspiration and community

On occasion, we create events where we showcase artisan products and serve beautiful food. We love these one-off evenings where we can all get inspired and share a space and a special moment. When we create events like this, it becomes a beautiful community. Food isn't just about nourishment – it is about fostering community and bringing people together under one roof.

OUR JAPANESE BREAKFAST

Every weekend since we opened CIBI in 2008, we have served a Japanese breakfast. This breakfast is the embodiment of our philosophy – nourishing, homely food that we simply want to enjoy eating and that's good for our bodies.

The typical Japanese breakfast consists of many different ingredients, including seasonal ones, together with a balanced amount of seasoning and flavour. They are thoughtfully prepared to nourish the body and feed the soul, with the right balance of ingredients and nutritional goodness. Traditionally, someone in the extended family – it tends to be the mother, grandmother or even great-grandmother – would prepare breakfast for the whole family. Often there are vegetables, salads, fish, tsukemono (pickled seasonal vegetables), as well as rice and miso soup. We may eat ten or more ingredients during the meal, with rice and miso soup as complementary dishes.

At CIBI, there is no focus on a particular ingredient, seasoning or diet. Instead, the focus is on preparing a nutritious and delicious meal. In the same way, there is no set order to eating a Japanese breakfast. Just dip in and eat it in whatever combination of dishes and flavours you like! Try it and you will really experience the goodness at the heart of Japanese food culture. Eat your Japanese breakfast with Japanese tea, which will give you the complete Japanese breakfast experience.

Traditional Japanese preserved foods such as nori (dried seaweed sheets), umeboshi (sour plum), natto (fermented soybeans), and tsukemono are good accompaniments for the rice in this breakfast.

ASSEMBLING A JAPANESE BREAKFAST

Soy sauce

Japanese tea (genmai-cha, hoji-cha or ryoku-cha)

Nori (dried seaweed) sheets

Umeboshi (sour plum)

Cabbage and ginger tsukemono (page 75)

Natto (fermented soybeans)

Ginger spinach ae-mono (page 30)

Sake-no-shio-yaki (grilled salmon fillet, see below)

Tamago-yaki (page 22)

Perfect Stovetop Rice (page 18)

CIBI egg and potato salad (page 120)

My Grandma's Miso Soup (page 20)

—

CIBIMEMO

Use 80 g (2¾ oz) salmon fillet per person. Season with salt and cook under the grill (broiler) at 180°C (350°F) for 5 minutes, or until cooked through.

BASIC RECIPES to MASTER

Japanese rice is an essential, beautiful part of Japanese cooking. Rice is grown throughout Japan, with different regions famed for the quality and flavour of their rice. The local rice is something we all grow up eating and treasuring. At my family home in Okayama, they still grow enough rice for family and friends. It's an important part of the meal; the glue that brings the different dishes – and the family – together. As a rule of thumb, use a ratio of 1 cup uncooked rice to 1 cup water.

HOW to MAKE PERFECT STOVETOP RICE

You can use this method with any tight-lidded saucepan or cooking pot. If you have a heavy, thick Japanese pot called a donabe, it makes the best rice.

SERVES 4–6

450 g (1 lb) white or brown medium-grain rice

1 Rinse the rice in cold water until the water runs clear – this will remove excess starch, ensuring the rice is nice and fluffy. Drain well.

2 Put the rice and 540 ml (18 fl oz) water in a saucepan and leave it to soak for at least 30 minutes (for brown rice, overnight is ideal).*

3 Put the lid on the saucepan and bring the rice to the boil. Once it boils, turn the heat down to low and cook for a further five minutes, then turn off the heat and let the grains steam, covered, for at least 10–15 minutes.

—

CIBIMEMO

* *To cook in a Japanese rice cooker (an electric one), switch it on after step 2.*

OUR FAVOURITE GRAIN MIXES

To get the most nutrition from grains and enjoy their textures, we like to combine and eat different kinds. These are our two iconic blends.

SERVES 4–6

WHITE GRAIN MIX

150 g (5½ oz) medium-grain brown rice

30 g (1 oz) dried soybeans

185 g (6½ oz) medium-grain white rice

45 g (1½ oz) white quinoa

RED GRAIN MIX

150 g (5½ oz) medium-grain brown rice

30 g (1 oz) dried soybeans

45 g (1½ oz) red azuki beans

185 g (6½ oz) medium-grain white rice

1 Soak the brown rice and soybeans (or, if you're making the red grain mix, the brown rice, soybeans and azuki beans) in water overnight (6–8 hours), then drain well.

2 Combine all the ingredients in a colander. Rinse them under cold water, then drain well.

3 Transfer the grains to a large saucepan, cover with 540 ml (18 fl oz) water, cover with a lid and bring to the boil. Once it boils, turn the heat down to low and cook for another five minutes, then turn off the heat and let the grains steam, covered, for at least 10–15 minutes.

—

CIBIMEMO

These are just some of our favourite grain mixes. Feel free to experiment! Other grains I recommend are millet, pearl barley, red rice, black rice, mung beans, black beans and broad beans.

HOW to MAKE DASHI and MISO SOUP

Miso shiru (miso soup) is an everyday soup that accompanies rice. Every family has its signature recipe, adding tofu, wakame, vegetables and more. It is the soul of Japanese meals – no matter where you are, you'll feel at home when sipping miso soup. You start by making dashi (stock), which adds wonderful flavour to miso soup and many other dishes in this book.

BASIC MISO SOUP

SERVES 4

150 g (5½ oz) silken tofu, cubed

2 tablespoons dried wakame seaweed flakes, soaked in water and drained

60 g (2 oz) white or red miso

2 tablespoons finely chopped spring onion (scallions), to garnish

DASHI

10 x 5 cm (4 x 2 in) piece of kombu

approximately 1 handful (7–8 g / ⅓ oz/1 cup) bonito flakes

Make the dashi

1   Combine 1 litre (34 fl oz/4 cups) water and the kombu in a large saucepan and simmer over a low heat. Just before the water starts to boil, remove the kombu.

2   Add the bonito flakes to the saucepan*. Cook over a low heat for 2 minutes and gently skim any foam from the surface using a fine-mesh strainer. Don't stir – doing so will make it bitter.

3   Turn off the heat and drain the stock through a fine-mesh sieve into a bowl. Discard the bonito flakes. Dashi will keep in the fridge for 2 days, and can be frozen in resealable bags.

Make the miso soup

1   Bring the dashi to the boil, add the tofu and wakame and cook for a couple of minutes over a low–medium heat.

2   Turn off the heat and blend the miso into the soup gently, using a miso koshi or fine-mesh strainer, or place the miso on a ladle, lower it into the soup and stir with chopsticks until the miso has dissolved.

3   Simmer the soup over a low heat. Just before it starts to boil**, turn the heat off. Garnish the soup with the spring onion and serve.

MY GRANDMA'S MISO SOUP

This is my grandma's miso soup recipe. We serve it as part of our Japanese breakfast – it's exactly what I used to eat when I was a kid. My grandma grows her own vegetables, and adds whatever is in season to the soup to make it wholesome and tasty.

SERVES 4

100 g (3½ oz) onion, finely sliced

70 g (2½ oz) carrot, cut into thin strips

150 g (5½ oz) potato, peeled and cubed

80 g (2¾ oz) daikon (white radish), cut into thin strips

1 litre (34 fl oz/4 cups) Dashi (see above)

100 g (3½ oz) silken tofu, cubed, or 30 g (1 oz) Japanese bean curd, cut into thin strips

60 g (2 oz) white or red miso

2 tablespoons dried wakame seaweed, soaked and drained

2–3 tablespoons finely chopped spring onion (scallions)

50 g (1¾ oz) snow peas, trimmed, blanched and finely sliced

1   Add the onion, carrot, potato and daikon to the dashi and cook over a medium heat for about 10 minutes, until the vegetables become soft. Add the tofu or bean curd.

2   Turn the heat off, then add the miso using a miso koshi (page 212) or a fine-mesh strainer to ensure the miso is blended evenly. Simmer the soup on a low heat, turning it off just before it starts to boil**.

3   Distribute the wakame and spring onion into individual soup bowls. Pour the miso soup over the top and arrange the snow peas on top.

—

CIBIMEMO

*   *Other classic Japanese dashi add-in options are dried shiitake mushrooms and niboshi (small dried anchovies). To make vegetarian dashi, leave out the bonito flakes.*

**   *Don't let your miso soup heat to above 95°C (200°F) – boiling miso soup is detrimental to its flavour. The best temperature at which to eat miso soup is around 75°C (170°F).*

DASHI

MISO SOUP

HOW TO MAKE TAMAGO-YAKI (JAPANESE OMELETTE)

Tamago-yaki is cooked in a special square pan (see page 212) that gives it a rectangular shape. We use a 15×15 cm (6×6 in) pan. Each Japanese family has a different recipe for this omelette, but this is simple and easy to make. It's a lot of fun, so enjoy it!

MAKES 2 ROLLS

6 eggs

1 teaspoon salt

1 tablespoon sugar

1 tablespoon mirin

1 tablespoon olive oil

maki-su (bamboo sheet for sushi rolls, optional)

1   In a bowl, combine 3 of the eggs, half a teaspoon of salt and half a tablespoon of sugar and mirin. Beat the eggs with either a fork or chopsticks. In a second bowl, repeat with the remaining eggs, salt, sugar and mirin.

2   Heat half a tablespoon of oil in a tamago-yaki or frying pan over a medium heat. Once the pan is hot, pour one-third of one of the egg mixtures into the pan. Once the egg has almost cooked, push it over to the side of the pan. If the pan is dry, add a little more oil.

3   Add another third of the egg mixture to the pan. Once its surface starts to cook, roll the first cooked egg portion over the new addition until you have a small egg roll. Repeat with the rest of the egg mixture, rolling the new additions over the growing egg roll.

4   Remove the egg roll from the pan and set it aside to cool. If you have a bamboo sheet (used for rolling sushi), roll it around the egg to help it keep its shape.

5   Add another half a tablespoon of oil to the pan and repeat the process with the other bowl of eggs, making a second tamago-yaki.

6   Once both tamago-yaki have cooled, slice them each into six 2–3 cm (¾–1¼ in) thick pieces crossways.

VEGETABLES

Vegetables are a big part of Japanese cuisine, and we love them dearly. They keep our bodies healthy and happy. At CIBI, we serve our lunch plate in classic Japanese style: two or three kinds of vegetables with a small portion of meat or fish. The recipes in this chapter are beautiful, versatile and great for sharing – serve them as a star dish on their own, or as an accompaniment to our seafood and meat options.

This is a handy recipe for when you can't be bothered cooking, but you know your body needs vegetables at the end of the day. I like to make this side dish in spring when asparagus is coming into season and tastes its best. When I'm super busy at work but need to make dinner for my lovely family and myself, I order some takeaway, then quickly cut and boil some vegetables and mix them with miso. That way, the meal is better balanced for body and soul. My sons love it.

ASPARAGUS with TOFU and LEMON MISO

SERVES 4–6

pinch of salt

200 g (7 oz) green beans

300 g (10½ oz, about 2 bunches) asparagus

1 zucchini (courgette), peeled into strips

150 g (5½ oz) momen (firm) tofu*, drained

120 ml (4 fl oz) Sweet Lemon Miso Sauce (page 207)

1 Bring a saucepan of water to the boil. Add the salt. Add the green beans and asparagus and let them cook for 1–2 minutes.

2 Drain the vegetables, then rinse them under cold running water to stop the cooking process. Once cooled, drain the vegetables well. Slice the beans in half lengthways, if desired.

3 On a serving plate, combine the cooked vegetables and zucchini strips. With your fingers, break the tofu up into crumbs and sprinkle over the vegetables. Drizzle over the sweet lemon miso sauce.

—

CIBIMEMO

* *The tofu we use for this recipe is momen (firm) tofu, which you can get from any supermarket or Asian grocer. Momen is firmer than silken tofu and easy to break up with your fingers. Broken up, it has a similar look and texture to ricotta cheese.*

This is one of the most refreshing salads we serve in summer. The seasoning is very simple, but the fresh ginger, sesame oil and salt are enough to make this dish complete. When we hold Saturday night markets at Minanoie, this dish is one of the first to disappear. It makes a great side dish and a tasty nibble to have with a beer after work. Though the flavours are quite Japanese, it's a good match with many different cuisines.

CRUNCHY VEGETABLE SALAD with BLACK SESAME and GINGER

SERVES 4–6

200 g (7 oz) broad (fava) beans

pinch of salt

100 g (3½ oz/⅔ cup) fresh peas, shelled

6–8 breakfast radishes, cut into quarters lenghtways

2 Lebanese (short) cucumbers, seeds removed and cut into 6–7 cm (2½–2¾ in) pieces

5 cm (2 in) piece of fresh ginger, finely sliced

2 teaspoons toasted black sesame seeds

2 teaspoons sea salt flakes, plus extra for blanching

2 teaspoons sesame oil

1 Bring a saucepan of water to the boil. Add the beans and the salt and cook for 3 minutes. Add the peas and cook for another minute.

2 Drain the vegetables, then rinse them under cold running water to stop the cooking process.

3 Squeeze the beans out of their pods and split them in half with your fingers.

4 In a large bowl, combine the radish, cucumber, beans, peas, ginger and sesame seeds. Season with the sea salt and sesame oil.

Houren-sou-no-ohitashi (blanched and marinated spinach with sauce) is a classic Japanese ae-mono (dressed vegetables with sauce), often served as a side or an appetiser alongside rice and soup. We serve this spinach ohitashi as part of our Japanese breakfast (page 16) on the weekend. It adds extra colour to the table and extra nutrition for your body. It's great with meat or eggs, too.

GINGER SPINACH AE-MONO

SERVES 2–4

250 g (9 oz) English spinach
pinch of salt
toasted white sesame seeds, to garnish
90 g (3 oz) Sesame Ginger (page 208)

1　Bring a saucepan of water to the boil. Add the salt and blanch the spinach for 30 seconds. Drain it, squeezing out any excess water.

2　Grind the sesame seeds with a mortar and pestle or use a sesame grinder (see page 213).

3　In a bowl, combine the spinach and sesame ginger and mix well. Sprinkle the sesame seeds on top.

Broccoli and miso go perfectly together – the broccoli soaks up the miso so nicely. Adding the texture of green beans and the freshness of daikon helps to balance everything out. We love soy-candied walnuts, which you can make separately and eat as a snack or side dish. They are great with French cheese!

BROCCOLI, SNOW PEAS, GREEN BEANS and DAIKON with MISO and SOY-CANDIED WALNUTS

SERVES 4–6

pinch of salt

1 broccoli head, trimmed
and cut into small pieces

200 g (7 oz) green beans,
cut in half on an angle

200 g (7 oz) snow peas (mangetout),
cut in half on an angle

¼ daikon (white radish), about 150 g
(5 fl oz), finely sliced

120 ml (4 fl oz) Sweet Miso Sauce
(page 207)

SOY-CANDIED WALNUTS

100 g (3½ oz/1 cup) walnuts

50 g (1¾ oz) brown sugar

1½ teaspoons tamari

1 Preheat the oven to 170°C (340°F).

2 To make the soy-candied walnuts, roast the walnuts in the oven for 12–15 minutes, then let them cool. In a saucepan, combine the brown sugar and tamari and cook over a high heat until thick and sticky, then add the walnuts and mix well. Spread the candied walnuts on a baking tray lined with baking paper and let them cool completely (they should be dry, not sticky). Break the nuts into small pieces with your fingers.

3 Bring a large saucepan of water to the boil. Add a pinch of salt and cook the broccoli for about 2 minutes. Add the green beans and cook for another minute, then add the snow peas and cook for a further 30 seconds.

4 Drain the vegetables and run them under cold water to stop the cooking process.

5 In a large bowl, mix together the green vegetables and the daikon. Add the sweet miso sauce and mix well, then sprinkle the candied walnuts over the top.

Nuta is a traditional Japanese side dish where ingredients are marinated in vinegar and miso. They catch a lot of octopus in the region where my grandma lives, so she makes her nuta with leeks and octopus. I've turned it into a simple vegetable dish by including seasonal spring vegetables that give it extra volume and nutrition. The miso sauce, with vinegar and a touch of karashi (Japanese mustard), gives the finished dish just the right amount of sweetness without taking away from the flavours of the vegetables. While traditional nuta is usually marinated for 15–30 minutes, this version is best served right away.

SPRING VEGETABLE NUTA

SERVES 4

4–6 small white radishes

pinch of salt

200 g (7 oz) broad (fava) beans, shelled

150 g (5½ oz) asparagus, cut in half on an angle

100 g (3½ oz/ ⅔ cup) fresh peas, shelled

1 small leek, finely sliced

130 g (4½ oz) kohlrabi, finely sliced

100 ml (3½ fl oz) Karashi Miso Sauce (page 207)*

1 Bring a saucepan of water to the boil. Add the radishes and salt and cook for 3 minutes, then add the beans and cook for another 2 minutes. Add the asparagus and cook for 30 seconds, then add the peas and cook for a further 30 seconds. Drain the vegetables, then rinse them under cold running water to stop the cooking process.

2 When the vegetables are cool, combine them in a bowl with the leeks and kohlrabi. Add the karashi miso sauce and mix well.

—

CIBIMEMO

* *Adding karashi (Japanese mustard) gives this dish a nice hint of spiciness. If you are sharing the dish with your kids, you may want to add less karashi to the sauce or leave it out altogether.*

*In early autumn, when the summer heat falls away and you feel like
you need to eat more vegetables, this is a good recipe to turn to.
Its greens, yellows and touches of brown are a nice celebration of
the time of year. The greens taste so good when they're cooked
lightly to retain their crunch, and they make your body feel so
happy. My kids love this, especially the greens and the corn.*

EARLY AUTUMN SALAD
with SESAME SAUCE

SERVES 4–6

pinch of salt

100 g (3½ oz) green beans,
cut in half on an angle

200 g (7 oz) broccoli,
cut into small florets

200 g (7 oz) broccolini,
cut diagonally into 3 cm (1¼ in) pieces

100 g (3½ oz) snow peas (mangetout),
trimmed

1 corn cob, shucked

olive oil, for frying

100 g (3½ oz) shimeji mushrooms,
broken into small pieces

95 ml (3¼ oz) Sesame Sauce
(page 208)

1 Bring a saucepan of water to the boil. Add the salt and blanch the
beans, broccoli, broccolini and snow peas for 1–2 minutes. Remove
the vegetables from the saucepan with a slotted spoon and set aside
in a large bowl.

2 In the same saucepan, boil the corn for 5–8 minutes, until cooked.
Drain and set aside to cool.

3 Add a splash of olive oil to a frying pan and sauté the mushrooms
over a medium heat for 2–3 minutes, or until tender. While they
cook, season them with salt and pepper.

4 Cut the corn off the cob.

5 In a large bowl, combine the greens, mushrooms and corn kernels
and drizzle the sesame sauce over the top.

This is one of my oldest recipes – a classic Japanese salad that I have been making for many, many years. I just love the combination of fresh tomato, cucumber, wakame seaweed, daikon and silken tofu mixed with a little bit of soy vinaigrette. On a hot day, I often feel like eating this salad and nothing else.

SUMMER SALAD with TOMATO, TOFU, CUCUMBER, DAIKON and SEAWEED

SERVES 4–6

10 g (¼ oz/¼ cup) wakame seaweed flakes

50 g (1¾ oz) mixed salad leaves

150 g (5½ oz) silken or momen (firm) tofu, cubed

2–3 medium tomatoes, cut into wedges*

1 Lebanese (short) cucumber or ½ telegraph (long) cucumber, deseeded and sliced

¼ daikon (white radish), about 150 g (5½ oz), finely sliced

75 ml (2½ fl oz) Soy Vinaigrette (page 208)

1 teaspoon toasted white sesame seeds

1 Soak the wakame flakes in a bowl of water for 5 minutes. Once they are rehydrated, drain them well.

2 In a large bowl or on a serving plate, combine all ingredients except the vinaigrette and sesame seeds. Handle the tofu gently, as it crumbles easily when stirred.

3 Drizzle the vinaigrette over the salad. Grind or sprinkle the sesame seeds over the top.

—

CIBI MEMO

* *We get many kinds of tomatoes in Australia that change with the seasons. Any variety will work in this salad. Try it with different tomato types to find the best match!*

We call this dish Japanese 'caprese' because its ingredients fit so perfectly with the ones in a classic Italian caprese. Instead of tomato, mozzarella and basil, we have tomato, tofu and shiso. It's a great way to enjoy tomatoes in summer, when they're at their best. You can drizzle it with olive oil, salt and pepper like an Italian caprese, or add soy vinaigrette to give it a more Japanese flavour. This is a great party starter and a beautiful vegan dish.

JAPANESE CAPRESE

SERVES 4

3 medium tomatoes, sliced into 1 cm (½ in) rounds

150 g (5½ oz) silken tofu

5–6 shiso leaves

2 tablespoons Soy Vinaigrette (page 208)

1 Arrange the tomato slices on a large serving plate.

2 Using a spoon, scrape out pieces of the tofu and arrange it on top of the tomatoes, then add the shiso leaves and drizzle over the vinaigrette. Season to taste with pepper.

—

CIBIMEMO

We sometimes use Goma-dare (Sesame Dressing) (page 208) instead of the soy vinaigrette for a different flavour.

The end of summer is my favourite time of year for seasonal produce. I particularly love heirloom tomatoes: I just eat them as is! I could stare at them all day long, they're so beautiful. Adding seasonal herbs and yuzu pepper dressing adds a hint of spice and elegance that makes the dish feel unique. When I first made it, I felt like I had discovered a whole new flavour.

HEIRLOOM TOMATO SALAD
with HERBS and YUZU PEPPER

SERVES 4

1 tablespoon chopped flat-leaf (Italian) parsley

1 tablespoon chopped coriander (cilantro)

1 tablespoon chopped mint

1 tablespoon chopped spring onion (scallions)

3–4 medium heirloom tomatoes, cut into wedges

60 ml (2 fl oz) Yuzu Pepper Dressing (page 211)

1   In a large bowl, combine the herbs, then add the tomatoes.

2   Pour the dressing over the top and mix well.

*When I see a freshly picked eggplant, this dish always springs to mind.
My grandma used to cook it for lunch when I came home from school on
Saturdays in summer, always using vegetables fresh from her garden.
It's nice to be able to share this dish with you – my grandma will be
happy, too. This is a great side dish to accompany meat or fish.*

SPICY MISO EGGPLANT

SERVES 4

**400 g (14 oz) eggplant (aubergine), cut
into 5 cm (2 in) wedges**

125 ml (4 fl oz/½ cup) olive oil

**100 g (3½ oz, about ½) green
capsicum (bell pepper),
sliced into thin strips**

**100 ml (3½ fl oz) Sweet Chilli Miso
Sauce (page 207)**

**toasted white sesame seeds,
to garnish (optional)**

1 Soak the eggplant in salted water for 10–15 minutes*. Drain well.

2 Heat the oil in a wok or large frying pan over a medium–high heat.
   Add the eggplant, stir well and cook for about 5 minutes, until
   soft. Add the capsicum, stir well and fry for 2 minutes, stirring
   occasionally. Stir in the sweet chilli miso sauce, then turn off
   the heat.

3 Transfer everything to a serving plate and sprinkle over the sesame
   seeds, if using.

—

CIBIMEMO

* *Soaking eggplant in salted water (1 pinch
   of salt to 1 litre [34 fl oz/4 cups] of water)
   for 10–15 minutes before you start
   cooking helps eliminate its harshness and
   improves its flavour. We call it aku-tori –
   'aku' means harshness or coarseness,
   and 'tori' means to take away or get rid of.*

We were introduced to this flavour combination in Paris. Mixing grated ginger with Lebanese tahini brought a new flavour into my kitchen. It's a great sauce to pair with many different ingredients, but this combination of eggplant and green beans is our favourite.

ROASTED EGGPLANT and GREEN BEANS with TAHINI GINGER DRESSING

SERVES 4–6

400 g (9 oz) eggplant (aubergine), cut into long wedges

75 ml (2½ fl oz) olive oil

pinch of salt

200 g (7 oz) green beans, trimmed

135 ml (4½ fl oz) Tahini Ginger Dressing (page 211)

coriander (cilantro) stalks and leaves, to garnish

1 Preheat the oven to 180°C (350°F).

2 Soak the eggplant wedges in a bowl of salted water for 10–15 minutes (see CIBI Memo on page 42). Drain well.

3 Arrange the eggplant in a roasting tin. Toss it with the olive oil, salt and pepper, and roast for 30 minutes.

4 Bring a saucepan of water to the boil. Add a pinch of salt and blanch the green beans for 1–2 minutes, depending on how crunchy you like them. Drain the beans well and let them cool, then cut them in half diagonally.

5 Once the eggplant has cooled, toss it with the green beans and dressing in a bowl. Transfer to a serving plate and garnish with the coriander stalks.

Ever since we opened Minanoie in 2012, this baked miso egg dish has been one of our signature breakfasts. I'm really happy with this great marriage between eastern and western flavours – everyone loves eggplant and miso (plus cheese). We use our nanbu-tekki (cast-iron) pans designed by Sori Yanagi for a sizzling, stylish oven-to-table service. You can bake and serve the dish in individual pans or one large pan for sharing.

BAKED MISO EGGS with ROASTED EGGPLANT and PUMPKIN

SERVES 4

500 g (1 lb 2 oz) eggplant (aubergine), sliced into 1 cm (½ in) thick rounds

pinch of salt

90 ml (3 fl oz) olive oil

250 g (9 oz) butternut pumpkin (squash), cubed

4 eggs

125 ml (4 fl oz/½ cup) thickened (pouring/whipping) cream

80 ml (2½ fl oz) Sweet Miso Sauce (page 207)*

2 tablespoons chopped spring onion (scallion)

150 g (5½ oz) provolone cheese, sliced

coriander (cilantro) leaves, to garnish

1 Preheat the oven to 170°C (340°F). Grease a heavy cast-iron pan or gratin dish (approx. 30×25 cm/12 in×10 in), or 4 individual cast-iron pans.

2 Soak the eggplant in salted water for 10–15 minutes (see CIBI Memo on page 42). Arrange the eggplant in a roasting tin, drizzle it with oil and season with salt and pepper. Roast for 20 minutes, until soft.

3 Steam the pumpkin in a double boiler for 5 minutes, or until cooked through.

4 Distribute the eggplant and pumpkin evenly in the cast-iron pan. Gently crack the eggs over the vegetables. Pour the cream and sweet miso sauce evenly over the dish, then sprinkle over the spring onion and top it all with the cheese.

5 Bake for 10 minutes, or until the cheese melts. Garnish with the coriander and serve hot, straight out of the oven.

—

CIBIMEMO

You can swap eggplant and pumpkin with other winter vegetables such as cauliflower, spinach, mushrooms and sweet potato.

* *Sweet miso sauce is great for marinating fish, meat or vegetables, as well as adding to salad dressings.*

*This is one of my simplest dishes. My kids love it, which makes
it really handy when they decide they're hungry and I want to make
a quick, filling and tasty dish. We serve it on toast for breakfast at
CIBI and often use it in our catering menu for canapés. At home,
we eat it with couscous or rice; it also makes a nice pasta sauce.*

EGGPLANT, TOMATO and CHICKPEA STEW

SERVES 4

400 g (14 oz) eggplant (aubergine), cubed

100 ml (3½ fl oz) olive oil

400 g (14 oz) tin diced tomatoes

400 g (14 oz) tin chickpeas, drained well

2 tablespoons chopped coriander (cilantro)

couscous or Perfect Stovetop Rice (page 18), to serve

1 Soak the eggplant in salted water for 10–15 minutes (see CIBI Memo on page 42), then drain well.

2 Heat the oil in a heavy-based frying pan over a medium–high heat. Add the eggplant and cook until soft, about 5 minutes.

3 Gently stir in the tomatoes, reduce the heat to medium–low and simmer for 15 minutes, until the liquid has reduced by one-third. Add the chickpeas and simmer for another 5 minutes. Season with salt and pepper to taste.

4 Add the coriander and stir gently. Serve with couscous or rice.

I remember summers as a kid, my mum would often ask me to quickly grab an eggplant and shiso from grandma's veggie garden in front of our house that she could cook for dinner. For me, it was just a normal thing to do. Today, it's a mantra: the freshest ingredients taste the best. Summer is the perfect time to make this tasty dish. Combining some of our most beloved Japanese summer ingredients and dressing them with our miso and sesame sauce completes the dish and the fullness of these seasonal flavours.

ROASTED EGGPLANT with CRUSHED TOFU, SHISO and MISO

SERVES 4

400 g (14 oz) eggplant (aubergine), sliced into rounds, then quartered

3–4 tablespoons olive oil

100 g (3½ oz) momen (firm) tofu, drained

4 medium shiso leaves, finely sliced, to garnish

MISO AND SESAME SAUCE

120 ml (4 fl oz) Sweet Miso Sauce (page 207)

2¹/₃ tablespoons ground toasted white sesame seeds

1   Preheat the oven to 180°C (350°F). Soak the eggplant in salted water for 10–15 minutes (see Cibi Memo on page 42), then drain well.

2   Put the eggplant in a roasting tin, brush it with the oil and season with salt and pepper. Roast for 20 minutes, or until soft.

3   To make the miso and sesame sauce, combine the ingredients in a bowl and mix well.

4   In a separate bowl, crush the tofu between your fingers to turn it into crumbs.

5   Plate the eggplant and top it with the tofu crumbs. Pour the sauce over the dish and garnish with the shiso.

*When you feel like cooking something different that will make your kids smile,
this is a good recipe. These tasty croquettes make a great afternoon snack or
finger food for a dinner party. I wanted to create croquettes without eggs and flour
(making them vegan and gluten-free), and this is what I came up with. Dressing
them with sesame seeds instead of panko crumbs and shallow-frying gives them
a nice, crunchy texture. They go well with a rich sesame sauce.*

PAN-FRIED JAPANESE PUMPKIN
and SPINACH CROQUETTES

MAKES 24 CROQUETTES

400 g (14 oz) kabocha (Japanese
pumpkin), peeled and cut into small
pieces

1 medium potato, peeled and cubed

2 pinches of salt

75 g (2¾ oz/1½ cups) English spinach,
chopped

2 teaspoons tamari

75 g (2¾ oz) rice flour

2 tablespoons cornflour (cornstarch)

½ teaspoon salt

¼ teaspoon sugar

50 g (1¾ oz/⅓ cup) toasted black
sesame seeds

50 g (1¾ oz/⅓ cup) toasted white
sesame seeds

100 ml (3½ fl oz) olive oil, for frying

150 ml (5 fl oz) Sesame Sauce
(page 208)

1 Steam the pumpkin for 5–10 minutes in a double boiler, until
   soft enough to mash.

2 Add the potato to a large saucepan of water with 1 pinch of
   salt and bring it to the boil. Cook for 10–15 minutes, until soft
   enough to mash.

3 In a bowl, mash the pumpkin and potato together.

4 Bring a saucepan of water to the boil. Add 1 pinch of salt and
   blanch the spinach for about 30 seconds. Drain under cold
   water to stop the cooking process.

5 Transfer the spinach to a blender, season with the tamari and
   blend into a paste.

6 In a bowl, combine the spinach paste, mashed vegetables,
   rice flour, cornflour, salt and sugar, and mix well.

7 On a plate, mix together the black and white sesame seeds.

8 Shape the batter into small balls, about 30 g (1 oz/2 tablespoons)
   each; you may need to lightly oil your hands to stop them from
   sticking. Roll the balls in the sesame seeds, then flatten them
   slightly with the palm of your hand.

9 Heat the oil in a frying pan over a medium–high heat and
   pan-fry the balls on all sides for a few minutes, until they are
   nice and golden.

10 Drizzle some sesame sauce on top before serving.

We cook this recipe year-round, both at CIBI and at home. Kabocha (Japanese pumpkin) tends to be very dense and sticky, so it tastes great when you steam or braise it. Roasting the pumpkin extracts its sweetness and intensifies its flavour, and adding sesame dressing gives it a special touch. You can make a big batch of this sesame dressing and keep it in the fridge for 2–3 months, as it is handy for many other dishes.

ROASTED JAPANESE PUMPKIN with GOMA-DARE

SERVES 4

300 g (10½ oz) kabocha (Japanese pumpkin), cut into small triangles, skin on*

olive oil, to coat

200 g (7 oz) broccoli, cut into small florets

200 g (7 oz) green beans, cut in half diagonally

toasted white sesame seeds, to garnish

150 ml (5 fl oz) Goma-dare (Sesame Dressing) (page 208)

1 Preheat the oven to 180°C (350°F).

2 Arrange the pumpkin on a roasting tin and drizzle with enough olive oil to coat evenly. Season with salt and pepper. Roast for 20 minutes, or until soft enough that you can easily pierce it with a fork.

3 In a large saucepan of water, combine the broccoli and green beans, cover them with water, bring to a boil and cook for 2 minutes.

4 Grind the sesame seeds with a mortar and pestle or use a sesame grinder (see page 213).

5 Plate the vegetables and drizzle the dressing over the top. Sprinkle the ground sesame seeds over to garnish.

—

CIBIMEMO

* If you cannot get kabocha, just use your favourite roasting pumpkin.

These Japanese stuffed vegetables are lots of fun to make and very simple, too! Once you've prepared the Tofu Mixture (page 97), all you have to do is hollow out the zucchini pieces, creating a hole to nestle the tofu in. You can reserve the zucchini flesh to use in a soup, pasta, risotto or stir-fried dish.

STUFFED ZUCCHINI with TOFU and SWEET LEMON MISO

MAKES 24 PIECES

250 g (9 oz) Tofu Mixture (page 97)

2–3 medium zucchini (courgettes)

1 tablespoon olive oil

120 ml (4 fl oz) Sweet Lemon Miso Sauce (page 207)

toasted white sesame seeds, to garnish

ao-nori (dried green seaweed), to garnish (optional)

1 Preheat the grill (broiler) to 170 °C (340 °F).

2 Make the tofu mixture following the recipe on page 97.

3 Cut the zucchini into 3 cm (1¼ in) rounds, then gently scoop out the flesh. You want to remove as much of the flesh as you can without scraping a hole straight through.

4 Heat the oil in a shallow frying pan and pan-fry the zucchini lightly over a medium heat, making sure to cook both sides. Don't pan-fry the zucchini for too long – doing so will change its texture, which may mean it falls apart when you try to stuff it.

5 Arrange the zucchini on a baking tray lined with baking paper. Using a small spoon, stuff some tofu mix into the hollow space in each zucchini. Brush them with some sweet lemon miso sauce.

6 Grill (broil) the zucchini until nicely browned, about 5 minutes.

7 Sprinkle over the sesame seeds and ao-nori, if using, to garnish.

I love really good pastry. We make our own at CIBI and use it for sweet tarts and savoury ones like this quiche. I just had to include this recipe – it is so good with its combination of buttery pastry, cream and a touch of salty miso. This makes a great brunch dish paired with a simple green leaf salad or Daikon and Mizuna Salad with Crispy Renkon (page 76).

SPINACH and MUSHROOM QUICHE

MAKES 8 MINI QUICHES

250 g (9 oz) Sautéed Mushrooms (page 64)

200 ml (7 fl oz) thickened (pouring/whipping) cream

2 eggs

100 g (3½ oz/1 cup) parmesan cheese, grated

100 g (3½ oz/1 cup) English spinach, blanched

60 ml (2 fl oz) Sweet Miso Sauce (page 207)

2 tablespoons snipped chives

PASTRY

1 egg yolk

2 teaspoons sugar

1 teaspoon salt

280 g (10 oz) unsalted butter, at room-temperature, plus extra for greasing

420 g (15 oz) plain (all-purpose) flour, sifted, plus extra for dusting

Make the pastry

1   In a small bowl, beat together the egg yolk and 75 ml (2½ fl oz) water. Add the sugar and salt and stir until combined. Refrigerate until ready to use.

2   In a large bowl, mash the butter until it is smooth and soft. Add the flour and mix well, until the mixture resembles crumbs.

3   Pour the egg mix into the flour. Mix well, until the pastry feels like soft skin.

4   Cover the pastry in plastic wrap and refrigerate for at least 2 hours or overnight to allow it to rest.

5   Preheat the oven to 180°C (350°F). Grease eight 12 cm (4¾ in) mini fluted tart tins with some butter.

6   Sprinkle a bit of flour on a large, flat board. Use a rolling pin to flatten the pastry into a sheet 3 mm (⅛ in) thick. Cut the pastry into 8 pieces. Line each tart tin with one of the pastry pieces. Use a fork to poke some small holes in the surface of the pastry, then chill the tins in the refrigerator for about 1 hour.

7   Fit some aluminium foil over the pastry and fill each tart tin with pastry weights. Bake for 20–25 minutes, or until golden brown. Remove the weights and foil and leave to cool on a wire rack.

Make the filling and assemble the quiches

1   Make the sautéed mushrooms following the recipe on page 64.

2   In a bowl, combine the cream, eggs, cheese and some salt and pepper and mix well.

3   Sprinkle the mushrooms and spinach into the mini tart tins. Pour the cream mixture over the mushrooms and spinach. Drizzle the sweet miso sauce over the top.

4   Bake the quiches for 20–25 minutes, until lightly brown. Garnish with the chives.

In Japan at the very end of autumn, you'll see lots of kaki (persimmon) hanging on the bare trees waiting to be picked. When I see them, I feel that winter is just around the corner. My grandma used to peel kaki harvested from her backyard and serve them fresh for dessert.

This is a revolutionary recipe for the way it combines three iconic Japanese ingredients: mushrooms, persimmon and chrysanthemum leaves. This combination is a beautiful marriage of flavours that makes you feel like you are eating the season. We eat chrysanthemum as a fresh salad – traditionally, they are often eaten in a hot pot or soup. This seasonal dish is a great one to serve as a side with all sorts of different meals. No dressing, as that way you can enjoy the ingredients' harmony.

AUTUMN SALAD with MUSHROOMS, PERSIMMON and CHRYSANTHEMUM

SERVES 4

3 tablespoons olive oil

150 g (5½ oz) shimeji mushrooms

100 g (3½ oz) oyster mushrooms

75 g (2¾ oz) enoki mushrooms

1 persimmon, cut into thin wedges

100 g (3½ oz) chrysanthemum leaves, to garnish (available from Asian grocers)

1 Heat the oil in a saucepan over a medium–high heat. Sauté the shimeji and oyster mushrooms for 4–5 minutes. When they are nearly cooked, add the enoki mushrooms and stir well. Turn off the heat and season with salt and pepper.

2 Once the mushrooms have cooled a little, mix them with the persimmon in a large serving bowl and garnish with the chrysanthemum leaves.

This is a fun recipe to make with your kids and a great party canapé.
Use medium-sized white or brown mushrooms and simply stuff them
with Chicken Soboro (page 160). So easy and tasty!

STUFFED MUSHROOMS with CHICKEN SOBORO and MAYO

MAKES 20

**20 mushrooms, preferably
6–8 cm (2½–3⅓ in) in diameter**

**150 g (5½ oz) Chicken Soboro
(page 160)***

3 tablespoons Japanese mayonnaise**

**2 tablespoons snipped chives, to
garnish**

1 Preheat the oven to 180°C (350°F). Line a baking tray with baking paper.

2 Using a small teaspoon, remove the mushroom stems to form a little crater. Stuff the craters with the chicken soboro – about 30–40 g (1–1½ oz) per mushroom.

3 Arrange the mushrooms on the baking tray, stuffed-side up, then dab some mayonnaise on top of each.

4 Bake the mushrooms for about 10 minutes, until their surfaces are brown. Sprinkle the chives on top and serve.

—

CIBIMEMO

* *If you prefer a vegetarian dish, you can stuff the mushrooms with Tofu Mixture (page 97) instead.*

** *If you cannot find Japanese mayonnaise, you can just use standard mayonnaise.*

We can get many different kinds of mushrooms in Australia these days, and this is a great way to make use of them. I sauté all sorts of Japanese mushrooms into an extravagant western-style poached egg breakfast infused with beautiful eastern twists. Toast your favourite bread from your local bakery, top it with this beautiful mushroom mix, and serve it with a Japanese onsen egg and a dash of soy sauce. Yum.

MUSHROOMS on TOAST with ONSEN EGGS

SERVES 4

4 eggs

4 slices sourdough bread

soy sauce, to garnish

SAUTÉED MUSHROOMS

80 ml (2½ fl oz) olive oil

150 g (5½ oz) Swiss brown mushrooms

100 g (3½ oz) shiitake mushrooms

150 g (5½ oz) shimeji mushrooms

50 g (1¾ oz) enoki mushrooms

2½ tablespoons red-wine vinegar

2 tablespoons chopped flat-leaf (Italian) parsley

1 tablespoon pink peppercorns

1 To make the onsen eggs*, bring 1 litre (34 fl oz/4 cups) water to the boil in a large saucepan. Once it boils, turn the heat off and add another 200 ml (7 fl oz) cold water, then gently lower the eggs, in their shell, into the saucepan using tongs. Cover with a lid and leave to sit for 12 minutes. Take the eggs out of the saucepan and set them aside to cool.

2 Heat the oil in a large frying pan over a medium–high heat. Add the Swiss brown and shiitake mushrooms and sauté for 5 minutes, stirring occasionally. If they get dry, add a little more oil. Once they are cooked through, add the shimeji mushrooms and cook for another 3 minutes. Add the enoki mushrooms and cook for a further 2 minutes.

3 Season the mushrooms with salt and pepper and add the red-wine vinegar. Quickly stir a few times to mix everything together.

4 Transfer the mushrooms to a bowl and mix in the parsley and peppercorns.

5 Toast the sourdough slices and arrange them on 4 plates. Top with some mushrooms, then crack an onsen egg over each. Add a dash of soy sauce onto the egg.

—

CIBIMEMO

* *Onsen eggs are a Japanese egg traditionally slow-cooked in the water of an onsen (Japanese hot spring). The egg white tastes like a delicate custard and the yolk comes out firm, but inside it remains uncooked. You can prepare them beforehand (a day ahead) and have them ready for breakfast.*

I love this mix of finely chopped vegetables tossed with our soy vinaigrette and goma-shio (sesame salt); I can't stop eating it! A little finely sliced celeriac lends a nice flavour to the slaw and sliced apple gives it a touch of sweetness. I love adding lots of chopped parsley as well. This is the perfect side for a big meat dish.

CIBI COLESLAW
with GOMA-SHIO

SERVES 4–6

500 g (1 lb 2 oz) Savoy cabbage, finely cut into thin strips

250 g (9 oz) red cabbage, finely cut into thin strips

80–100 g (2¾–3½ oz) fuji or similar apple

juice of ½ lemon

150 g (5½ oz) daikon (white radish), finely cut into thin strips

100 g (3½ oz) cucumber, finely cut into thin strips

70–80 g (2½–2¾ oz) carrot, finely cut into thin strips

150 g (5½ oz) celeriac, finely cut into thin strips

2 tablespoons chopped flat-leaf (Italian) parsley

150 ml (5 fl oz) Soy Vinaigrette (page 208)

GOMA-SHIO (SESAME SALT)*

100 g (3½ oz/⅔ cup) black sesame seeds

50 g (1¾ oz) salt

1 To make the goma-shio, heat a small frying pan over a medium–low heat and add the sesame seeds. Pan-fry them for 7–8 minutes until fragrant. Add the salt and fry for another 3–5 minutes. Pour the mixture into a mortar and pestle and grind well.

2 Combine the Savoy and red cabbage and soak them in cold water for 10–15 minutes. Drain well.

3 Cut the apple into thin strips and place in a small bowl. Squeeze the lemon juice over it and mix well.

4 In a large bowl, mix together the vegetables, apple and parsley. Pour over the soy vinaigrette and mix well. Sprinkle the goma-shio on top and serve.

—

CIBIMEMO

* *I make my goma-shio with a 2-to-1 sesame-to-salt ratio. It keeps in an airtight container for up to 3 months and is a great seasoning for rice, salad, meat, fish or even as a nice table salt.*

This is a very simple, cleansing winter salad. In Japan, we often eat hakusai (Chinese cabbage) cooked or pickled, but this recipe uses it raw: just mix it with kohlrabi and mandarins and season well with good salt and dark sesame oil. I love the combination of these vegetables and mandarins, which make for a colourful match. This dish goes nicely with braised fish and meat.

HAKUSAI, KOHLRABI
and MANDARIN SALAD

SERVES 4

400 g (14 oz) hakusai (Chinese cabbage), thinly sliced

100 g (3½ oz) kohlrabi, peeled and thinly sliced

2 mandarins, peeled and separated into segments

1 tablespoon chopped flat-leaf (Italian) parsley

2½ tablespoons dark sesame oil

½ tablespoon salt

1   In a bowl, mix together the cut vegetables and mandarin. Season with the sesame oil and salt and mix well.

Several years ago at CIBI, I wanted to serve something quite Japanese, but with CIBI style – something everyone would love to eat. This okonomi-yaki is totally unique and gluten-free, lighter than the usual Japanese okonomi-yaki. We use lots of fresh sweet corn mixed with finely shredded cabbage. This recipe makes four okonomi-yaki, but you can make smaller ones as a snack or larger ones as a full meal.

CABBAGE and CORN OKONOMI-YAKI

MAKES 4

300 g (10½ oz) Savoy cabbage, finely shredded

pinch of salt

250 g (9 oz) corn, about 2 cobs, or use frozen corn kernels

200 g (7 oz) rice flour

200 ml (7 fl oz) Dashi (page 20)

½ teaspoon salt

2 eggs

30 g (1 oz/¼ cup) chopped spring onion (scallion)

4 cm (1½ in) piece of fresh ginger, grated or finely chopped

1 tablespoon olive oil

CIBI'S OKONOMI-YAKI SAUCE

2½ tablespoons soy sauce or tamari

2 tablespoons rice vinegar

1 tablespoon sugar

1 tablespoon finely chopped spring onion (scallion)

1 teaspoon sesame oil

1 To make the sauce, combine all the ingredients in a small bowl and mix well.

2 Soak the cabbage in cold water for 10–15 minutes, then drain well.

3 If you are using corn cobs, bring a saucepan full of water to a boil. Add the pinch of salt and the corn and cook for 5–8 minutes. Drain and set aside to cool. Once the corn has cooled down, cut the kernels off the cob.

4 In a bowl, whisk together the flour, dashi and salt until well mixed.

5 In another bowl, beat the eggs with a fork or chopsticks.

6 In a large bowl, combine the cabbage, corn (boiled or frozen), spring onion, ginger, eggs and flour mixture. Mix well with a fork or chopsticks.

7 Heat the oil in a frying pan over a medium–high heat. Pour a quarter of the batter in, forming a round pancake. Reduce the heat to medium–low and cook until they are crisp and brown, about 5–7 minutes on each side. Repeat to make three more pancakes. If necessary, add more oil to the pan.

8 Plate the pancakes and brush some sauce over the top before serving.

I love this combination so much. The white and light green of the fennel complements the light yellow and salmon pink of the grapefruit, and it tastes just as beautiful as it looks. This salad goes nicely with baked fish, a mild curry or a meat dish.

GRAPEFRUIT, FENNEL and CUCUMBER SALAD with HONEY MUSTARD DRESSING

SERVES 4–6

100 g (3½ oz, about ½) pink grapefruit, peeled and separated into segments

100 g (3½ oz, about ½) grapefruit, peeled and separated into segments

1 Lebanese (short) cucumber or ½ telegraph (long) cucumber, cut into thin rounds, then quartered

400 g (14 oz) fennel bulb, halved and thinly sliced

1 tablespoon finely chopped flat-leaf (Italian) parsley

90 ml (3 fl oz) Honey Mustard Dressing (page 211)

1 Cut each grapefruit segment in half on an angle.

2 Cut the cucumber rounds into quarters.

3 In a bowl, combine the grapefruit, cucumber, fennel and parsley. Add the dressing and mix well.

Since we moved back to Australia in 2005, the vegetable and fruit varieties available here have gotten better and better. When I first met the Australian nashi pear, the taste wasn't as good as the amazing Japanese nashi, but these days the quality is consistently good. Nashis are refreshing, juicy and mildly sweet. They add a nice freshness to this salad, while the three different herbs add sharpness and depth. I love the gradations of green colour happening in this dish, too.

NASHI PEAR, COS LETTUCE and HERB SALAD

SERVES 4–6

2 baby or 1 regular cos (romaine) lettuce

1 nashi pear*

2 tablespoons finely chopped flat-leaf (Italian) parsley

2 tablespoons finely chopped coriander (cilantro)

2 tablespoons finely chopped mint

2 tablespoons extra-virgin olive oil

juice of ½ lemon

1　Wash and dry the lettuce well. Cut it into 5–6 cm (2–2½ in) squares.

2　Cut the nashi in half. Remove its core and finely slice the flesh.

3　In a large bowl, combine the lettuce, nashi and herbs. Season with some salt and pepper, the oil and lemon juice and mix well.

—

CIBIMEMO

* *If you cannot find nashi, you can use another type of pear.*

This is another cabbage dish I can't stop eating. You're likely to find yourself picking at these tsukemono (pickles) while you're preparing dinner, they are so good. They have a beautiful ginger flavour, and just the right amount of sourness. You can eat the tsukemono with other Japanese dishes, but it is a good match for many different cuisines. I often serve it with Braised Koji Pork Belly (page 170).

CABBAGE and GINGER TSUKEMONO

SERVES 4–6

450–500 g (1 lb–1 lb 2 oz) cabbage, cut into 3–4 cm (1¼–1½ in) squares

⅔ medium carrot, finely cut into strips

½ telegraph (long) cucumber, finely sliced

1 tablespoon sugar

1 teaspoon salt

170 ml (5½ fl oz/⅔ cup) olive oil

3 cm (1¼ in) piece of fresh ginger, finely sliced

10 black peppercorns

1 dried chilli, finely sliced

170 ml (5½ fl oz/⅔ cup) rice vinegar

1 In a bowl, combine the cabbage, carrot, cucumber, sugar and salt and mix well.

2 In a small saucepan, heat the oil, ginger, peppercorns and chilli over a medium–high heat. Once the oil is hot, pour it on top of the vegetables.

3 Pour the rice vinegar onto the vegetables and mix well. Transfer the salad into a resealable bag, lay it on a flat tray with a weight on top (such as a plate or a pot) and refrigerate for 6–8 hours or overnight to pickle before serving.

This version of daikon salad mixes finely sliced daikon with candy beets and some mizuna leaves. Adding crispy renkon (lotus root) makes it a very special and tasty dish. I add yuzu pepper to the mayo dressing, which is the perfect match for these vegetables.

DAIKON and MIZUNA SALAD with CRISPY RENKON

SERVES 4

100 g (3½ oz) renkon (lotus root)

1 tablespoon vinegar

50 g (1¾ oz) cornflour (cornstarch)

olive oil, for deep-frying

250 g (9 oz) mizuna

1 small to medium candy beet, washed and thinly sliced

200 g (7 oz) daikon (white radish)

175 ml (6 fl oz) Yuzu Pepper Mayo Dressing (page 211)

1 To make the crispy renkon, peel the renkon and cut it into 5 mm (¼ in) rounds. Soak them in a mixture of the vinegar and 500 ml (17 fl oz/2 cups) water for at least 10 minutes to stop them from changing colour. Drain well.

2 Lightly season the renkon with salt and pepper. Coat both sides with the cornflour, gently shaking off any excess.

3 Heat the oil in a deep-fryer or large, heavy-based saucepan (fill the pan to a depth of approx. 3 cm/1¼ in) over a medium–high heat. Deep-fry the renkon until crispy and light-brown.

4 In a large bowl, combine the renkon with the mizuna, candy beet and daikon. Drizzle over the mayo dressing and mix well.

We have been serving this east-meets-west dish at our parties and functions for a long time. Believe it or not, daikon and prosciutto go together really well. It is very simple, fresh and light. This is a perfect canapé, entrée or snack dish to enjoy with your aperitif.

DAIKON, PROSCIUTTO and WATERCRESS WRAPS

MAKES 24

300 g (10½ oz) daikon (white radish), finely sliced and cut into matchsticks

50 g (1¾ oz) watercress, washed and dried

180–200 g (6½–7 oz, about 12 slices) prosciutto, cut in half on an angle

SOY VINEGAR

3 tablespoons rice vinegar

2 tablespoons soy sauce

1 To make the soy vinegar, mix together the vinegar and soy sauce in a bowl.

2 Add the daikon to the vinegar sauce, mix well, and let it marinate for 5–10 minutes. Drain the daikon.

2 Place a small amount of daikon and 1–2 sprigs of watercress on the edge of a slice of prosciutto. Wrap it up into a cigar-like stick. Repeat with the remaining ingredients.

In this recipe, miso soup becomes a hero dish rather than a side. I sometimes see people drink the broth in miso soup and leave the fillings behind, but this soup is definitely meant to be eaten. Miso soup is like a Japanese version of minestrone – lots of vegetables, and made with mum's (or grandma's) love. Just as each family or region in Italy uses different minestrone ingredients and flavours, Japanese miso soup varies too. I put lots of wintery root vegetables in mine. If you add small pieces of sliced pork, it becomes a ton-jiru (buta-jiru), or pork soup.

'EAT YOUR SOUP' MISO SOUP
with ROOT VEGETABLES

SERVES 4

100 g (3½ oz) konnyaku
(Japanese taro)*

1 medium onion, finely sliced

1 medium carrot, quartered and sliced

220 g (8 oz, about 1 medium)
potato, peeled and cut into small cubes

150 g (5½ oz, about ¼) daikon
(white radish), quartered and sliced

4 shiitake mushrooms, finely sliced

1.6 litres (54 fl oz) Dashi (page 20)
or vegetable stock

1 turnip, cubed

120–150 g (4½–5½ oz, about ⅓) sweet
potato, cubed

200 g (7 oz) hakusai (Chinese
cabbage), cut into 3 cm
(1¼ in) squares

1 piece of Japanese bean curd,
rinsed with hot water, drained and cut
into 1 x 3 cm (½ x 1¼ in) strips

100 g (3 ½ oz) red miso paste

2 tablespoons chopped spring onion
(scallion), to garnish

2 tablespoons sesame oil, to garnish

1 teaspoon shichimi-togarashi
(Japanese seven spice), to garnish

1 Bring a saucepan of water to the boil and cook the konnyaku for 5 minutes to remove its harshness. Drain it and let it cool down enough to handle. Break it into 2 cm (¾ in) pieces with your fingers.

2 In a large stockpot, combine the onion, carrot, potato, daikon, mushrooms and konnyaku. Add the dashi and bring it to the boil. Cook for 15–20 minutes over a medium–high heat, until the ingredients are soft and cooked through. Add the turnip and sweet potato and cook for another 5 minutes. Add the hakusai and bean curd and cook for a further 5 minutes.

3 Remove the stockpot from the heat and add the miso. If you have a miso strainer, it is very handy at this stage. Otherwise, scoop the miso onto a ladle, slowly lower it into the soup and stir it gently with chopsticks until the miso is completely dissolved. Reduce the heat to low and return the stockpot to cook for another few minutes, then turn off the heat.

4 Divide the soup between 4 bowls and garnish with spring onion. Drizzle over the sesame oil and sprinkle the shichimi-togarashi on top.

——

CIBIMEMO

* *Konnyaku is a Japanese taro plant. In processed form, it is available in little packets, in water. These packets are often dark grey in colour and gooey like jelly. Konnyaku is rich in fibre and is often said to cleanse your stomach. I love its texture, and adding it to this soup makes us feel healthy. If you cannot find konnyaku, that's totally fine; you can make beautiful miso soup without it.*

When the weather is cold, especially in winter, we always feel like eating something to warm us up, which often means soup or hot pot. When I make soup in winter, it has to have lots of vegetables to recharge me and my family. I usually take whatever is available in the fridge, chop it up and put it in a pot to make the soup. I always use a chunk of daikon because it is so good and my son loves it – he says the taste reminds him of his great grandma's daikon dish at Oshou-gatsu (New Year).

DAIKON and ROOT VEGETABLE SOUP with FARRO

SERVES 4

1 litre (34 fl oz) Chicken Stock
(page 124)

5 x 5 cm (2 x 2 in) piece of kombu,
cut into small pieces*

150 g (5½ oz) daikon (white radish),
peeled and cubed

1 medium onion, cut into wedges

1 medium potato, peeled and cubed

1 medium carrot, cubed

1 celery stalk, chopped

3–4 shiitake mushrooms, sliced

100 g (3½ oz) farro

¼ cabbage, cut into squares

¼ cauliflower, cut into small florets

2 Swiss chard leaves, cut into squares

2 tablespoons chopped spring onion
(scallion)

2 tablespoons chopped flat-leaf
(Italian) parsley

1　In a large stockpot, combine the chicken stock, 600 ml (20½ fl oz) water, kombu, daikon, onion, potato, carrot, celery and shiitake mushrooms, and bring to the boil. Once boiling, reduce the heat to medium and cook the vegetables for 10–15 minutes, until they become soft. Skim off any foam that rises to the surface.

2　Add the farro, cabbage and cauliflower and cook for another 10 minutes. Add the Swiss chard and cook for a further 5 minutes.

3　Season the soup with salt and pepper to taste. Just before you turn off the heat, stir in the spring onion and parsley.

—

CIBIMEMO

*　*Kombu is usually used for flavouring stock, but isn't eaten with it. I include it in this recipe to add extra umami to the chicken stock, but also because it is high in minerals and very healthy.*

We use yuzu in dressings quite a lot at CIBI. It adds a very nice citrus touch, but one that is quite different from lemon or orange. We love using seasonal vegetables in our kitchen – that is the best way to enjoy them and experience the season. We pick heirloom carrots and yellow and green beans at the very beginning of spring. This warm salad is quite simple to make – just lightly cook the vegetables and dress them with the yuzu miso, which also makes a great dipping sauce for vegetable sticks.

HEIRLOOM CARROTS, YELLOW and GREEN BEANS with YUZU MISO

SERVES 4

400 g (14 oz) heirloom carrots

100 g (3½ oz) yellow beans, trimmed

100 g (3½ oz) green beans, trimmed

2 sprigs chervil

YUZU MISO

2 tablespoons white miso

2 tablespoons yuzu jam*

1 Bring a saucepan of water to the boil. Add a pinch of salt, then add the carrots and cook for 3 minutes. Add the yellow and green beans and boil for 30 seconds, until lightly cooked. (Make sure not to overcook the vegetables or they will lose their texture.) Drain and rinse the vegetables under cold water to stop the cooking process. Drain well again.

2 To make the yuzu miso, combine the miso and yuzu jam in a small bowl and mix well.

3 Plate the vegetables and drizzle the yuzu miso over the top. Garnish them with the chervil leaves.

—

CIBIMEMO

* *You can usually find yuzu jam at Japanese or Korean grocers, or at large Asian grocers.*

I first made this dish when we had our food philosophy exhibition in 2011, and since then it has become a regular dish on the menu at CIBI. Namasu is a type of pickle – you use amazu (a mixture of vinegar and sugar) to marinate the vegetables, sometimes with yuzu peels or chilli. Our namasu requires an additional step: you marinate the veggies again with sesame sauce, which makes the flavour even more rounded and lovely. Namasu is usually a mixture of daikon and carrot, but purple carrot makes the dish a beautiful light purple. Very nice.

DAIKON and PURPLE CARROT NAMASU

SERVES 4–6

120 ml (4 fl oz) Amazu (page 211)

200 g (7 oz, about ½) daikon (white radish), thinly sliced and cut into strips

150 g (5½ oz) purple carrot, thinly sliced and cut into strips

toasted white sesame seeds, to garnish

SWEET SESAME SAUCE*

3½ tablespoons toasted white sesame seeds

80 ml (2½ fl oz/⅓ cup) unhulled tahini

2 tablespoons mirin

1 tablespoon rice vinegar

1 tablespoon sugar

¼ teaspoon salt

1　In a large bowl, mix the amazu with the daikon and let it marinate for at least 30 minutes.

2　To make the sweet sesame sauce, combine all the ingredients together in a small bowl and mix well.

3　Drain the daikon, then mix it with the purple carrot and the sweet sesame sauce and let it marinate for 20–30 minutes.

4　Grind the sesame seeds with a mortar and pestle or use a sesame grinder (see page 213). Sprinkle them over the top of the dish and enjoy.

—

CIBIMEMO

*　*Sweet sesame sauce tends to become rather thick, but as soon as you have marinated the vegetables with it, the liquid from the daikon and carrot creates a perfect consistency.*

When I feel like eating dark-coloured vegetables, I always think about this salad and our CIBI Coleslaw (page 66). I love this dish, which we serve as a side with our Slow-cooked Chicken with Green Olives (page 164). Using daikon makes this French-style salad somehow seem quite Japanese. Lime juice and zest are refreshing and add another touch of green.

BEETROOT and DAIKON SALAD with LIME

SERVES 4

2 tablespoons pumpkin seeds

200 g (7 oz) beetroot (beets), finely sliced and cut into thin strips

150 g (5½ oz) daikon (white radish), finely sliced and cut into thin strips

60 g (2 oz) carrot, finely sliced on an angle and cut into thin strips

2 tablespoons finely chopped flat-leaf (Italian) parsley

zest and juice of 1 lime

1   In a small saucepan, toast the pumpkin seeds over a low heat for about 5 minutes, until fragrant.

2   In a bowl, mix the beetroot, daikon and carrot.

3   Add the pumpkin seeds, parsley, lime zest and lime juice to the bowl with the vegetables. Season them with salt and pepper and mix well to combine.

I came up with this combination when I was thinking up a new winter menu for Minanoie, where our aim is to make all of our vegetable dishes vegan and gluten-free. This aim results in recipes like this one that are quite unique. We use soy milk, rice flour and olive oil to make a white sauce – a step away in flavour from the milk, flour and butter combination most of us are used to. Layering this soy milk white sauce over winter vegetables creates an amazing, healthy gratin that's not too rich and is visually very beautiful. This unconventional dish won't disappoint you.

WINTER GRATIN with BEETROOT and ROOT VEGETABLES

SERVES 4–6

1 beetroot (beet)

pinch of salt

100–120 g (3½–4½ oz) potato, peeled and cubed

3 tablespoons olive oil, plus extra for greasing

150 g (5½ oz) onion, cut into thin wedges

70 g (2½ oz) carrot, cubed

250 g (9 oz) butternut pumpkin (squash), cubed

100 g (3½ oz) turnip, cubed

70 g (2½ oz) sweet potato, cubed

200 g (7 oz) cauliflower, chopped

80 ml (2½ fl oz/⅓ cup) Sweet Miso Sauce (page 207)

1 tablespoon chopped flat-leaf (Italian) parsley, to garnish

GRATIN SAUCE

500 ml (17 fl oz/2 cups) soy milk

2 tablespoons olive oil

4 tablespoons rice flour or cornflour (cornstarch)

1 To make the gratin sauce, warm the soy milk in a saucepan over a medium–high heat. Combine the oil and flour in a separate saucepan and whisk over a medium heat for about 1 minute. Slowly add the warm milk to the flour mixture and whisk until the sauce thickens, about 5–10 minutes. Season to taste with salt and pepper and turn off the heat.

2 In a saucepan, cover the beetroot with water and boil over a high heat until cooked through, about 20–30 minutes. Once it's cool enough, peel and cut it into thin wedges.

3 Place the potatoes and a pinch of salt in a saucepan with water. Bring to the boil, then simmer for 10 minutes, or until you can pierce them easily with a skewer.

4 Preheat the oven to 180°C (350°F). Grease a large gratin dish with oil.

5 Add the oil to a large, heavy-based stockpot or saucepan and sauté the onions over a medium heat until they are soft and translucent. Add the carrot and cook for 5 minutes, then add the butternut, turnip and sweet potato and cook for another 5 minutes. Add the cauliflower, stirring well. Add in 125 ml (4 fl oz/½ cup) water and simmer, covered, over a medium–low heat for 5 minutes.

6 When the vegetables are cooked, drain them. Combine all vegetables in a large bowl with half of the gratin sauce and mix well.

7 Pour the vegetables into the gratin dish. Spread the remainder of the gratin sauce over the vegetables and drizzle the sweet miso sauce over the top. Bake for 30 minutes until nice and golden. Garnish with chopped parsley and serve.

We served this dish to our friends when Kato-san of Kamawanu (a Japanese traditional fabric company in Tokyo) visited us for our collaborative exhibition in the spring. This recipe was created and served to complement and celebrate both food and tenugui (see page 213) – how both celebrate and honour the seasons in their different ways. The raw vegetables are finely sliced and arranged on a plate like carpaccio, then drizzled with this amazing yuzu pepper dressing. The combination is just perfect, producing a delicious WOW.

SEASONAL VEGETABLE CARPACCIO

SERVES 4–6

200 g (7 oz) heirloom carrots

150 g (5½ oz) asparagus

200–220 g (7–8 oz) zucchini (courgettes)

50–60 g (1¾–2 oz) radishes

3 tablespoons Yuzu Pepper Dressing (page 211)

a handful of chervil leaves to garnish

1 Using a vegetable peeler, cut the carrots vertically into long, thin strips. Slice the asparagus and zucchini the same way, then the radishes.

2 Arrange the sliced vegetables on a large serving plate. Season them very lightly with salt and pepper.

3 Drizzle the dressing over the vegetables and garnish with chervil.

—

CIBIMEMO

To truly enjoy this dish, I recommend you use a vegetable peeler to ensure the vegetables are very thin and that you plate them in nice, thin layers.

This is one of the recipes I'm proudest of. It's a filling winter dish that recharges the batteries. The cooked hijiki (seaweed) and su-renkon (pickled lotus root) make this a real east-meets-west dish. I enjoy when different flavours merge into a totally new dish. You'll be amazed at how well it goes with any kind of cuisine.

ROASTED JERUSALEM ARTICHOKES and BEANS with COOKED HIJIKI and SU-RENKON

SERVES 4–6

300 g (10½ oz) Jerusalem artichokes, cubed

300 g (10½ oz) potatoes, cubed

olive oil, to coat

pinch of salt

100 g (3½ oz) edamame, shelled

100 g (3½ oz) tinned red kidney beans

100 g (3½ oz) tinned chickpeas

100 g (3½ oz) tinned lentils

3 tablespoons extra-virgin olive oil

SU-RENKON*

50 g (1¾ oz) renkon (lotus root)

1 teaspoon salt

3 tablespoons rice vinegar

1 tablespoon sugar

COOKED HIJIKI

25 g (1 oz) dried hijiki seaweed

1½ tablespoons sugar

1 tablespoon mirin

1 tablespoon sake

1 tablespoon soy sauce

1 To make the su-renkon, peel the renkon, thinly slice it and soak it in water to prevent it from changing colour. Bring a saucepan of water to the boil. Add half the salt and the renkon and boil for 3–4 minutes, or until cooked through. (Don't overcook it, as it will ruin the su-renkon's fresh and crunchy texture.) Drain and cool the renkon. In a saucepan, bring the vinegar, sugar and the remaining salt to the boil. When the sugar has dissolved, turn off the heat. Add the cooked renkon and let it pickle.

2 To make the cooked hijiki, rehydrate the hijiki seaweed for 10–15 minutes in just enough water to cover it. Combine all the cooked hijiki ingredients – including the soaking water – in a saucepan and simmer over a medium heat for 20–25 minutes, until the liquid disappears. If any liquid is left, make sure to drain it away.

3 Preheat the oven to 180°C (350°F).

4 Arrange the Jerusalem artichokes and potatoes in a roasting pan. Coat them in olive oil, season with salt and pepper, and roast them for 30 minutes, until nice and golden.

5 Bring a small saucepan of water to the boil. Add the pinch of salt and boil the edamame for 1 minute.

6 Arrange the kidney beans, chickpeas and lentils in a roasting tin. Warm them in the oven for 5–7 minutes.

7 In a large bowl, combine the artichokes, potatoes, edamame, beans, chickpeas and lentils with the su-renkon and 3 tablespoons of the cooked hijiki (the rest can be eaten with rice, potato salad or a green salad). Mix in the extra-virgin olive oil and season with salt and pepper.

—

CIBIMEMO

* *Su-renkon (pickled lotus root) should be prepared at least 1 hour before serving, though making it a day ahead will ensure it is well pickled. It will last for 1 week in a sealed container in the refrigerator. You can eat it as is or with a green leaf salad.*

I love roasting sweet potato and cauliflower, so I decided to bring the two together. Yoghurt and chives balance things out really well. Its colours make it a perfect winter dish, and it is lovely served as a side to our Slow-cooked Beef Cheek (page 176) and Koji Pork Belly (page 170).

ROASTED SWEET POTATO and CAULIFLOWER with YOGHURT and CHIVE DRESSING

SERVES 4–6

350 g (12½ oz) sweet potato, cubed

350 g (12½ oz) cauliflower, cut into small florets

100 ml (3½ fl oz) olive oil

70–90 g (2½–3 oz) cucumber, cut into quarters lengthways and thinly sliced

YOGHURT AND CHIVE DRESSING

150 g (5½ oz) natural Greek yoghurt

2 tablespoons extra-virgin olive oil

1 tablespoon lemon juice

1 tablespoon snipped chives

1   Preheat the oven to 180°C (350°F).

2   Arrange the sweet potato and cauliflower on a baking tray, season with some salt and pepper and roll them in the oil. Roast them for 30 minutes, or until the vegetables are soft. Allow them to cool a little while you make the dressing.

3   In a small bowl, combine all the dressing ingredients and mix well. Season with salt and pepper to taste.

4   In a large bowl, combine the roasted vegetables with the cucumber and the dressing and mix them together well.

We've had this dish on the menu at CIBI since we opened in 2008. The tofu mixture in this classic Japanese dish is at the heart of many of our tofu dishes. You can make small patties for kids or to serve at parties, or large patties to turn into a meal. You can make them into any size or shape, so you can entertain yourself and your guests with your creativity. Tofu patties go well with Daikon and Mizuna Salad with Crispy Renkon (page 76).

CIBI TOFU PATTIES
with TERIYAKI SAUCE

SERVES 4–6

100 g (3½ oz) cornflour (cornstarch)

100 ml (3½ fl oz) olive oil

TERIYAKI SAUCE

80 ml (2½ fl oz/1/3 cup) tamari

80 g (2¾ oz) sugar

3 tablespoons mirin

3 tablespoons sake

1 tablespoon cornflour (cornstarch)

TOFU MIXTURE

500 g (1 lb 2 oz) fresh tofu, drained well

2 tablespoons olive oil

200 g (7 oz) onion, finely chopped

180 g (6½ oz) carrot, finely chopped

1/3 cup dried, sliced shiitake mushrooms, soaked in water, drained and finely chopped

3 tablespoons chopped spring onion (scallion)

4–5 cm (1½–2 in) piece of fresh ginger, grated or finely chopped

2 tablespoons tamari

1 tablespoon sesame oil

1 tablespoon cornflour (cornstarch)

Make the teriyaki sauce

1 In a saucepan, combine the tamari, sugar, mirin, sake and 250 ml (8½ fl oz/1 cup) water and boil for 3–5 minutes.

2 In a separate bowl, mix together the cornflour and 2 tablespoons water. Turn off the heat, then add the cornflour mixture to the saucepan. Simmer on a low heat, stirring, until the cornflour has dissolved and the sauce thickens nicely.

Make the tofu mixture

1 Wrap the tofu block in a paper towel and place it on a flat tray. Place a small chopping board on top, just big enough to cover the tofu, and put a weight on top of the board, in order to extract as much water as possible. Leave it to drain for at least 30 minutes.

2 In a frying pan, heat the oil over a medium heat and sauté the onion and carrot until tender and soft, about 5–10 minutes. Season with salt and pepper and leave to cool.

3 Break the tofu up into small pieces with your fingers and add to a bowl with the onions, carrot, mushrooms, spring onion, ginger, tamari, sesame oil and cornflour. Mix very well to form the tofu patty mixture.

4 Divide the mixture into patties that weigh around 150–170 g (5½–6 oz) each. Toss each patty ball gently between your hands to get the air out of it (making it less likely to fall apart), then shape it.

Cook the tofu patties

1 Coat the patties in cornflour. Pour the oil into a frying pan and pan-fry the patties over a low–medium heat for about 5 minutes per side, until they are nicely brown and firm.

2 Turn the heat off, then pour the teriyaki sauce into the pan and mix gently. Serve immediately.

During winter in Japan, around Oshou-gatsu (New Year), there is always pickled turnip on the dining table. There is also a famous pickled turnip dish, called senmai-zuke (sliced pickled turnip) in Kyoto. This recipe uses pickled turnip as a salad ingredient, combining it with apple and bean curd. I recommend preparing the pickled turnip a day before so it tastes even better!

PICKLED TURNIP, APPLE, BEAN CURD and MIZUNA SALAD

SERVES 4

10 x 15 cm (4 x 6 in/1 sheet) Japanese bean curd

100 g (3½ oz) red apple (Fuji, if available), thinly sliced and quartered

50 g (1¾ oz) mizuna*

3 tablespoons Honey Mustard Dressing (page 211)

PICKLED TURNIP

60 ml (2 fl oz/¼ cup) rice vinegar

1 tablespoon sugar

¼ teaspoon salt

200 g (7 oz) turnip, thinly sliced and cut into quarters

3 x 3 cm (1¼ x 1¼ in) piece of kombu, cut into thin strips

¼ teaspoon dried chilli flakes

1 In a small saucepan, combine the vinegar, sugar and salt and simmer over a low heat until the sugar has dissolved.

2 In a small bowl, combine the turnip, kombu and chilli flakes. Pour over the vinegar mixture, mix well and let it marinate. Prepare it at least 30 minutes before, though making it a day ahead will ensure the turnip is well pickled.

3 Rinse the bean curd under hot water to remove any excess oil. Dry it lightly with paper towel.

4 Place the bean curd in a frying pan over a medium–low heat and pan-fry on both sides for a few minutes, until lightly brown and crispy. Remove it from the pan and let it cool, then slice it into 1 x 5 cm (½ x 2 in) pieces.

5 In a large bowl, mix the bean curd, apple, mizuna and pickled turnips. Drizzle over the honey mustard dressing.

—

CIBIMEMO

You can store the pickled turnip in the fridge for up to 2 weeks. It's great to eat as is, but also great to mix with other fresh salads. Use the pickle juice as a dressing with extra-virgin olive oil.

* If you cannot find mizuna, any mixed salad leaves or iceberg lettuce will work here.

This vegetarian miso gratin uses a selection of winter vegetables and tofu, creating a wholesome, nutritious winter dish that will warm your body and recharge you. It's a simple, tasty way to look after your health.

WINTER MISO GRATIN with CAULIFLOWER, TOFU and MUSHROOMS

SERVES 4

butter, for greasing

300 g (10½ oz) cauliflower, cut into small florets

½ tablespoon olive oil

1 king oyster mushroom, thinly sliced

25 g (1 oz/½ cup) panko breadcrumbs*

20 g (¾ oz) parmesan cheese, grated

1 tablespoon finely chopped flat-leaf (Italian) parsley

150 g (5½ oz) momen (firm) tofu, cubed

100 ml (3½ fl oz) thickened (pouring/whipping) cream

3 tablespoons Sweet Miso Sauce (page 207)

1 Preheat the oven to 180°C (350°F). Butter the surface of a casserole dish or cast-iron pan.

2 Bring a saucepan of water to the boil. Add the cauliflower and boil for a few minutes, until lightly cooked.

3 Heat the oil in a small frying pan over a medium–high heat and sauté the mushroom for 2–3 minutes, or until cooked through. Season with salt and pepper.

4 In a small bowl, mix together the breadcrumbs, cheese and parsley.

5 Arrange the cauliflower, mushroom and tofu in the casserole dish. Drizzle over the cream and sweet miso sauce. Spread the breadcrumb mixture evenly over the vegetables and bake the gratin for 20 minutes, until nice and brown.

—

CIBIMEMO

* *If you are looking for a gluten-free recipe, you can cook this gratin without the breadcrumbs. Just sprinkle cheese and parsley on top and bake! It's also nice with English spinach if you want to add an extra dose of greens.*

GRAINS and SANDWICHES

In addition to rice, the heart and soul of Japanese cooking, we want to introduce you to the many different kinds of grains and sandwiches we serve at CIBI and eat at home. From classic Japanese noodles to a delicious barley salad and a swordfish sandwich, these recipes are versatile and full of goodness. Grains provide good energy – eating them alongside fish, meat and vegetables makes for a happy, balanced diet, while sandwiches are the perfect choice for a quick and delicious lunch.

Sushi has long been an iconic Japanese dish. There are many types – nigiri sushi, maki-sushi, chirashi-sushi and more – but this temaki sushi is probably the most common form cooked and eaten in Japanese homes. I often describe temaki as being like Mexican tacos, with nori and rice in place of corn tortillas. Just fill it with your favourite toppings, dip it in soy sauce and eat. Your kids can help you prepare it, too. It's a great home party meal. I'd like to introduce it to as many people as possible, because it is simple to prepare and you can have a really fun time making it with family and friends. I have listed many topping choices, but you can pick them to suit your guests and family or the occasion.

Every New Year, we have a Shin-nen-kai (New Year Party) with our team at CIBI, and we always have temaki sushi. Our Japanese team members show our Australian and international team members how to make and eat it, what combinations of toppings work best, and more. This dish has become our team bonding meal.

TEMAKI SUSHI

SERVES 4–6

10–15 nori (seaweed) sheets (21 x 19 cm/ 8¼ x 7½ in), cut into four squares

100 g (3½ oz) sashimi-grade salmon, cut into 8–12 pieces, 5 mm (0.2 in) thick

100 g (3½ oz) sashimi-grade tuna, cut into 8–12 pieces, 5 mm (0.2 in) thick

8–12 cooked prawns (shrimp)

1 Lebanese (short) cucumber, cut into 10 cm (4 in) sticks

2 avocados, cut into 1.5 cm (½ in) wedges

12 shiso leaves

30 g (1 oz/2 cups) mixed salad leaves

4 tablespoons Japanese mayonnaise

soy sauce, for dipping

wasabi, to garnish*

pickled ginger, to garnish

SU-MESHI (VINEGARED RICE)

450 g (1 lb) medium-grain white rice

60 ml (2 fl oz) rice vinegar

2 tablespoons sugar

1 teaspoon salt

TERIYAKI CHICKEN

3 tablespoons soy sauce

3 tablespoons sugar

3 tablespoons mirin

3 tablespoons sake

300 g (10½ oz, about 2) boneless, skinless chicken thighs

½ tablespoon olive oil

2 Tamago-yaki (page 22)

Make the su-meshi

1 Rinse the rice in a bowl and drain well. Leave it for about 30 minutes to let the rice absorb the excess water.

2 Put the rice in a saucepan, pour in 530 ml (18 fl oz) water and cover. Cook the rice over a high heat until steam starts escaping. Turn the heat to low, cook for another 5 minutes, then turn off the heat and let it stand for at least 10 minutes. Make sure not to remove the lid as it rests; this is an important step in the rice cooking process (page 18). You want it to be just al dente, as it softens when the vinegar is mixed in.

3 While the rice is cooking, combine the rice vinegar, sugar and salt in a bowl and mix well until the sugar and salt have dissolved.

4 Transfer the cooked rice into a sushi-oke (see page 213) or big bowl. While the rice is still hot, pour the rice vinegar mixture over it and stir well. It is important to make this a quick and gentle stir: you don't want to squash or overmix the rice – this can make it too sticky.

5 Cool the rice under a fan until nice and shiny. You can use a Japanese paper or fabric fan for this, an electric fan, or even a magazine or newspaper.

Make the teriyaki chicken

1 To make the teriyaki sauce, mix the soy sauce, sugar, mirin and sake in a small saucepan and cook over a high heat until the liquid has reduced by one-third and is fairly thick.

2 Season the chicken with salt and pepper. Heat the oil in a small frying pan over a medium–high heat, then add the chicken slices. Cook until both sides are nice and crisp, about 5–8 minutes.

3 Just before you turn off the heat, pour the sauce over the chicken and stir to coat well.

4 Cool the chicken and cut it into 10 cm (4 in) strips.

Make the Tamago-yaki

1 Follow the instructions on page 22.

Set up the table and assemble the sushi

1 Once all of the ingredients are cooked and prepared, arrange them nicely on your favourite plates. Serve the sushi rice in a bowl with a rice paddle or spoon. Lay the nori squares on a plate.

2 To eat, take a piece of nori and put it on your palm. Spread a small quantity of sushi rice evenly over the nori. Pick one or two of your favourite ingredients and place them on the nori diagonally, so that they are facing two of its corners. Add a small amount of wasabi for garnish, if you like.

3 Roll the nori sheet, rice and toppings together to form a cone. Dip it in soy sauce and enjoy! You can serve the temaki sushi with a side of pickled ginger.

—

CIBIMEMO

* *Wasabi is Japanese horseradish often used with sushi. It is very flavoursome but can be extremely hot and spicy – a little goes a long way.*

In Japan, we have a dish called hiyashi-chuka that's like a cold ramen without any soup. If you are exhausted from the heat and don't feel like eating dinner, this is the dish to get you interested in food and get your body feeling back to normal. On a hot summer's day, my family eats this cold salad version of hiyashi-chuka for dinner. It goes well with any of your favourite fresh summer vegetables – I have included some of our favourites, but choose whichever ones you like best.

HIYASHI-CHUKA–STYLE COLD RAMEN SALAD

SERVES 4

4 Soy Eggs (page 160)

200 g (7 oz) Poached Chicken (page 124), sliced

1 small carrot, cut into thin strips

½ telegraph (long) cucumber, sliced diagonally and cut into thin strips

50 g (1¾ oz/1 cup) English spinach, blanched, drained and cut into 5 cm (2 in) lengths

¼ yellow capsicum (bell pepper), cut into thin strips

2 tablespoons dried kikurage (black ear mushrooms), soaked in warm water and thinly sliced (optional)

1 tablespoon soy sauce

1 tablespoon sesame oil

2 teaspoons mirin

1 tablespoon toasted white sesame seeds

800 g (1 lb 12 oz) fresh or frozen ramen noodles, or 360–400 g (12½–14 oz) dried ramen noodles*

2–3 tomatoes, cut into thin strips

1 handful mixed salad leaves

2 tablespoons Goma-dare (Sesame Dressing) (page 208)

150 ml (5 fl oz) Nanban sauce (page 208)

KARASHI MAYONNAISE

1 teaspoon karashi powder**

3 tablespoons Japanese mayonnaise

1 Make the soy eggs following the instructions on page 160.

2 Make the poached chicken following the instructions on page 124.

3 To make the karashi mayonnaise, whisk together the karashi powder and 1 teaspoon water to form a paste, then mix it into the mayonnaise.

4 In a bowl, combine the carrot, cucumber, spinach, capsicum and mushrooms with the soy sauce, sesame oil and mirin and mix well. Let the vegetables marinate for 10–15 minutes, then sprinkle over the toasted sesame seeds.

5 Bring a large saucepan of water to the boil and cook the noodles, following the packet instructions. Once they are cooked until just al dente, drain and run them under cold water to stop the cooking process and wash off excess gluten.

6 In a large, shallow bowl, combine the noodles with the marinated vegetables, the tomato and the salad, then arrange the chicken on top.

7 Pour the goma-dare (sesame dressing) over the poached chicken and the nanban sauce over the noodle salad. Serve the karashi mayonnaise on the side.

—

CIBIMEMO

* *If you can find good fresh ramen noodles, that's great, but dried noodles are fine too!*

** *If you can't get karashi powder, you can always find Japanese karashi paste at an Asian grocer (where you can also find wasabi paste). Otherwise, you can use hot English mustard as a substitute.*

The older you get, the more often your body misses what you ate in your childhood. Out of all the different noodles, I love udon noodles the most simply because I grew up in one of Japan's best-known udon regions. This recipe is easy to prepare – perfect for when you don't have time to cook, but want a quick and healthy lunch at home.

I used to try and eat at least one good udon noodle meal on every trip back to Japan, but have done so less since we started serving this dish. Very funny, but it is that good! Our broth is made with poached chicken stock instead of fish stock and only a small dash of soy sauce, which makes the dish less Japanese, but very CIBI.

UDON NOODLE SOUP

SERVES 2

2 Onsen Eggs (page 64)

400 g (14 oz) fresh
or frozen udon noodles or
180–200 g (6½–7 oz) dried
udon noodles *

40 g (1½ oz) Poached Chicken
(page 124), sliced

30 g (1 oz) English spinach,
blanched and cut into 5 cm
(2 in) lengths, to serve

2 tablespoons finely chopped spring
onion (scallion), to serve

4 lemon slices, to serve

¼ teaspoon yuzu pepper

CHICKEN BROTH

300 ml (10 fl oz) Chicken Stock
(page 124)

1 tablespoon soy sauce

pinch of salt

1 For the chicken broth, combine the chicken stock and 200 ml (7 fl oz) water in a large saucepan and bring it to the boil. Add the soy sauce and the pinch of salt. Adjust the flavour of the broth with more salt and soy sauce, if needed.

2 Make the onsen eggs following the instructions on page 64.

3 Bring a large saucepan of water to the boil. Cook the udon noodles, following the packet instructions. When the noodles are cooked, drain them well.

4 Divide the noodles between two serving bowls. Pour 250 ml (8½ fl oz/1 cup) broth over each.

5 Place an onsen egg in the middle of each bowl. Top the noodles with the chicken, spinach, spring onion and lemon slices. Sprinkle over a little bit of yuzu pepper and serve.

—

CIBIMEMO

This soup is very easy to make if you have all the ingredients ready in advance. If you don't have time to prepare the chicken stock or poached chicken, you can get the stock from the grocery store, or substitute poached chicken with salt-and-peppered, pan-fried chicken.

* This common Japanese noodle is made from flour and varies from region to region. The most common udon noodle is from the Sanuki region in Shikoku Island. You can make fresh udon noodles at home or buy them frozen or dried at a Japanese grocer.

We have been serving our soba salad since we opened CIBI in 2008. When I created this dish, I wanted to add a touch of western flavour so that it became a cafe-like dish as well as a CIBI dish. Many of our regulars come in just for this salad. This is a simpler version that you can cook at home anytime. All you really need in your cupboard is soba noodles, soy sauce and lemon!

CIBI SOBA SALAD

SERVES 2–4

30 g (1 oz, or 10 x 10 cm/4 x 4 in) Japanese bean curd

200 g (7 oz, about 2 bunches) dried soba noodles

2 handfuls mixed salad leaves

90 g (3 oz, around 6) cherry tomatoes, halved

½ avocado, cubed

1 tablespoon finely chopped spring onion (scallion)

1 tablespoon toasted white sesame seeds

SOBA DRESSING

2 tablespoons extra-virgin olive oil

1½ tablespoons lemon juice

1 tablespoon tamari

OLIVE RELISH

100 g (3½ oz) pitted green olives, finely chopped

1 tablespoon olive brine

juice of 1 lemon

3 tablespoons extra-virgin olive oil

1 To make the olive relish, combine the olives, olive brine, lemon juice and oil in a bowl. Season with freshly ground black pepper to taste and mix well.

2 To make the soba dressing, combine all of the ingredients in a small bowl with 50 ml (1¾ fl oz) water and mix well.

3 Drain the bean curd and rinse it with hot water to remove any excess oil. Dry it lightly with paper towel. Pan-fry both sides in a frying pan over a low–medium heat until light brown and crispy. Remove it from the pan and let it cool, then slice it into 1 x 5 cm (½ x 2 in) rectangles.

4 Bring a large saucepan of water to the boil. Add the soba noodles and cook, following the packet instructions, until they are just al dente. Drain the noodles and run them under cold water to stop the cooking process and wash off excess gluten. This will help give the noodles a nice texture.

5 Arrange the salad leaves on plates.

6 In a large bowl, combine the noodles, tomatoes, avocado, bean curd, spring onion, sesame seeds and dressing and mix well. Top the salad on each plate with a helping of the noodle mixture. Garnish each with 1 teaspoon of the olive relish and serve the rest of the relish on the side.

*I love introducing Japanese ingredients to western-style dishes to create a
sensational harmony. Pearl barley, beetroot and feta is a classic combination,
and adding meaty shiitake mushrooms gives it a great texture. The colour
of this dish is stunning too. It makes a great lunch or side dish.*

PEARL BARLEY SALAD with SHIITAKE MUSHROOMS, BEETROOT and FETA

SERVES 4

200 g (7 oz) pearl barley

1 medium beetroot (beet)

6 tablespoons olive oil

250 g (9 oz) shiitake mushrooms, quartered

100 g (3½ oz/⅔ cup) feta cheese, crumbled

½ medium carrot, cut at an angle and sliced into thin strips

2 tablespoons finely chopped flat-leaf (Italian) parsley, plus extra leaves, to garnish

3 tablespoons extra-virgin olive oil

juice of ½ lemon

1 teaspoon sea salt flakes or rock salt*

1   Bring a saucepan of water and the pearl barley to the boil. Turn the heat down to medium and cook for 15 minutes, or until the barley is al dente. Drain well and set aside to cool.

2   Bring a saucepan of water and the beetroot to the boil. Reduce the heat to medium and cook for 15 minutes, or until soft. The beetroot is cooked when you can easily pierce it with a fork or chopstick. Drain the beetroot and peel it, then trim the roots and stems, and cut it into thin wedges. Halve the wedges on an angle.

3   Heat the olive oil in a frying pan and sauté the mushrooms over a high heat until nice and soft, about 5–7 minutes. Season with salt and pepper and allow them to cool.

4   In a bowl, combine the pearl barley, beetroot, mushrooms, feta cheese, carrot and parsley. Add the extra-virgin olive oil, lemon juice, salt and some pepper to taste and mix well.

—

CIBIMEMO

*   *Using good salt is always the key to success when it comes to flavour. We use sea salt flakes in our salads, or rock salt.*

This is a summer version of our popular Udon Noodle Soup (page 109). Kake (kake-ru) means 'to pour' in Japanese, though we don't use as much broth here as we do for our noodle soup. The combination of niku-miso (minced meat cooked with miso) and eggplant is so good. This simple dish is all you need for an interesting and restorative lunch.

KAKE UDON NOODLES with NIKU-MISO and EGGPLANT

SERVES 2

½ medium eggplant (aubergine), cut in 1 cm (½ in) wheels*

60 ml (2 fl oz/¼ cup) olive oil

2 Onsen Eggs (page 64)

400 g (14 oz) fresh or frozen udon noodles or 180–200 g (6½–7 oz) dried udon noodles

2 tablespoons chopped spring onion (scallion), to garnish

2 tablespoons chopped shiso leaves, to garnish

1 small handful ito-togarashi (angel hair chilli), to garnish (optional)**

¼ teaspoon shichimi-togarashi (Japenese seven spice), to garnish (optional)

NIKU-MISO

1 tablespoon olive oil

200 g (7 oz) minced (ground) pork

1 tablespoon grated fresh ginger

1½ tablespoons Sweet Chilli Miso (page 207)

1 tablespoon toasted white sesame seeds

BROTH

250 ml (8½ fl oz/1 cup) Chicken Stock (page 124)

1 teaspoon soy sauce

1 teaspoon mirin

1 Preheat the oven to 180°C (350°F). Soak the eggplant in salted water for 10–15 minutes to get rid of some of its harshness (see the CIBI Memo on page 42). Drain them well and dry with paper towel. Lay the eggplant on a baking tray, then pour over the oil, season with salt and pepper, and roast for 15–20 minutes, until soft.

2 Make the onsen eggs following the recipe on page 64.

3 To make the niku-miso, heat the oil in a frying pan over a medium heat. Add all the ingredients and mix well to combine. Simmer for 10 minutes, or until the liquid has evaporated.

4 To make the broth, pour the chicken stock and 70 ml (2¼ fl oz) water into a saucepan and bring to the boil. Add the soy sauce and mirin, and season with salt. Cook for 3 minutes.

5 Bring a stockpot of water to the boil. Cook the noodles following the packet instructions, then drain well and run under cold water to stop the cooking process and to wash off excess gluten.

6 Transfer the cooked udon noodles to two noodle bowls. Pour the broth over the noodles. If you like cold broth, cool it before serving or make it a day ahead and keep it in the fridge. Top with the spring onion, shiso leaves, niku-miso, roasted eggplant, onsen eggs and ito-togarashi and shichimi-togarashi, if using.

—

CIBIMEMO

* *You can always substitute the eggplant in this recipe with other seasonal vegetables, if you like.*

** *Ito-togarashi (sil gochu, also called angel hair chilli) comes in fine strands that are mild, fruity and have a gentle warmth. This chilli complements any dish, from grilled fish to soups and canapés.*

On a hot summer day, this is a great dish to cool you down. You can eat this harusame (vermicelli noodle) salad as a main or side dish, whichever you like. Make sure to add lots of summer vegetables so your diet is balanced and to help your body recover from the heat. Adding fresh ginger is key to this recipe – and to keeping healthy during the summer months. You can substitute the vegetables with whatever is in season, or add to the vegetables listed below.

HARUSAME SALAD with SUMMER VEGETABLES, EDAMAME and KIKURAGE MUSHROOMS

SERVES 4–6

100 g (3½ oz) harusame (vermicelli noodles)

1 tomato, cut into 5–6 cm (2–2½ in) strips

½ medium carrot, finely sliced at an angle and cut into thin strips

⅓ cucumber, finely sliced at an angle and cut into thin strips

¼ red capsicum (bell pepper), finely cut into thin strips

4 dried kikurage (black ear mushrooms), soaked in warm water and finely sliced

50 g (1¾ oz) edamame, shelled and boiled

2–3 cm (¾–1¼ in) piece of fresh ginger, finely sliced and cut into thin strips

120 ml (4 fl oz) Soy Vinaigrette (page 208)

coriander (cilantro) leaves, to garnish

toasted white sesame seeds, freshly ground, to garnish

1   Soak the harusame in a large bowl of warm water until soft and transparent. This step is important, as soft noodles will absorb the dressing and taste nicer. Drain them well.

2   In a large bowl, combine the harusame, tomato, carrot, cucumber, capsicum, kikurage, edamame and ginger and mix well.

3   Add the soy vinaigrette and mix well.

4   Plate the salad and garnish with some coriander and ground sesame seeds.

—

CIBIMEMO

Make sure the vegetables are finely sliced and cut into thin, noodle-like strips so the dish will have the perfect look and texture. Your veggie measurements don't have to be precise for this recipe: just add as much as you like.

This is one of my oldest recipes, and everyone's favourite. We serve it as part of our CIBI Japanese breakfast (page 16). For this sandwich, I add lots of eggs, gouda cheese and broccoli to the potato salad, then mix it well with Japanese mayonnaise. When you grill it, the cheese starts melting and tastes really good.

CIBI EGG and POTATO SANDWICH

MAKES 4 SANDWICHES

700–800 g (1 lb 9 oz–1 lb 12 oz) potatoes, peeled and cubed

1 teaspoon salt

100 g (3½ oz/1⅔ cups) broccoli, blanched and finely chopped

4 hard-boiled eggs, peeled and finely chopped

1 tablespoon finely chopped flat-leaf (Italian) parsley

100 g (3½ oz) gouda cheese, cubed

100 g (3½ oz) Japanese mayonnaise

8 slices sourdough

2 tablespoons dijon mustard

1   In a large saucepan, combine the potatoes and salt. Cover with water and bring to the boil. Cook the potatoes until they are soft enough to mash.

2   Drain the potatoes, transfer them to a bowl and mash them well (there should be no lumps). Leave to cool. Season the mash with salt and pepper and mix well.

3   Add the broccoli, eggs, parsley, cheese and mayonnaise to the bowl with the potatoes and mix well. Taste and adjust the seasoning with salt, pepper and mayonnaise.

4   Spread the egg and potato mix on 4 of the sourdough slices. Spread ½ tablespoon of the dijon mustard on each of the other 4 slices, then assemble the sandwiches.

5   Toast the sandwiches in a sandwich press until the bread is nice and brown and the gouda melts. If you don't have a sandwich press, you can heat a frying pan and toast them on both sides, until the cheese starts oozing out.

—

CIBIMEMO

This filling is also great on its own! My kids love it as is, and we often serve it as a side to our Barbecue Wagyu Beef (page 173).

This is one of our favourite sandwiches of late. The juicy, yummy fillings are perfect throughout the year. Me-kajiki (swordfish) is common in Japan, often eaten as sashimi as well as deep-fried, teriyaki and meuniere. Tatsuta-age–style swordfish (swordfish marinated in tamari and ginger, then shallow-fried) goes beautifully with egg and mayo tartare, smashed edamame and salad greens – these hints of Japanese flavour make this dish quite special. I love its layered colours: brown (from the tatsuta-age), yellow (from the egg tartare), bright green (from the edamame) and deep green (from the salad greens).

TATSUTA-AGE–STYLE SWORDFISH SANDWICH with EGG TARTARE and MASHED EDAMAME

MAKES 4 SANDWICHES

60 ml (2 fl oz/¼ cup) soy sauce

60 ml (2 fl oz/¼ cup) sake

2 tablespoons grated fresh ginger

400 g (14 oz) swordfish, cut into 4 pieces*

100 g (3½ oz) cornflour (cornstarch)

100 ml (3½ fl oz) olive oil

8 slices sourdough

mixed salad leaves

¼ telegraph (long) cucumber, sliced

2 tablespoons dijon mustard

EGG TARTARE

3 hard-boiled eggs, finely chopped

3 tablespoons Japanese mayonnaise

1 tablespoon chopped Italian (flat-leaf) parsley

1 tablespoon lemon juice

1 teaspoon capers

1 teaspoon caper juice

MASHED EDAMAME

150 g (5½ oz) shelled edamame (fresh or frozen), cooked**

60 ml (2 fl oz/¼ cup) extra-virgin olive oil

juice of ¼ lemon

1   To make the egg tartare, gently mix all of the ingredients together in a bowl. Season with salt and pepper to taste.

2   To make the mashed edamame, put all of the ingredients in a blender and blend to a coarse paste. Season with salt and pepper to taste.

3   Combine the soy sauce, sake and ginger in a flat enamel tray. Coat both sides of the swordfish in the marinade and let it sit for 10 minutes. Pour the cornflour onto a separate plate and coat both sides of the swordfish with it, shaking off any excess.

4   Heat the oil in a frying pan over a medium heat and shallow-fry the swordfish for 5–7 minutes, until crispy and brown.

5   If you like a toasted sandwich, you can toast the bread at this stage.

6   Arrange some salad leaves on top of 4 slices of sourdough, then a couple of cucumber slices, then one-quarter of the egg tartare. Top with a piece of swordfish, then with one-quarter of the mashed edamame. Spread dijon mustard on the last 4 slices and assemble the sandwiches.

—

CIBIMEMO

*   *Salmon is nice, too, if you can't find swordfish.*

** *Edamame are soybeans harvested when they are still green and in the pod. They are often served boiled and salted as a starter with beer. You can find frozen edamame at Asian grocers.*

We've had this simple, classic sandwich on the menu at CIBI pretty much from the beginning. You can use the poached chicken breast from this recipe on salads or with noodles, too. We use leftover chicken stock in all sorts of ways – it is sensational in risotto.

POACHED CHICKEN SANDWICH
with LEMON MAYO

MAKES 4 SANDWICHES

8 slices sourdough
mixed salad leaves
80 g (2¾ oz) pecorino cheese, sliced*

POACHED CHICKEN AND CHICKEN STOCK
500 g (1 lb 2 oz) boneless,
skinless chicken breast
100 ml (3½ fl oz) white wine

LEMON MAYONNAISE
150 g (5½ oz) Japanese mayonnaise
zest and juice of ½ lemon

1 To make the poached chicken (and chicken stock), first season the chicken with salt and pepper. Transfer it to a heavy casserole dish, laying it down nice and straight. Pour the white wine over the chicken, then add 1 litre (34 fl oz) water. Bring to the boil, skim off any white foam that floats to the surface, and turn the heat down to low**. Cover and simmer for 15 minutes, until the chicken is cooked through. Turn off the heat and let it sit for about 15 minutes.

2 Take the chicken out and let it cool, then slice it into thin pieces. (We use the leftover chicken stock for our udon noodle recipes, pages 117 and 109; you can freeze the stock in resealable bags).

3 To make the lemon mayonnaise, combine the ingredients in a small bowl and mix well.

4 Lay some salad leaves on top of 4 slices of sourdough, then add about 100 g (3½ oz) of chicken on top of each. Spread on some lemon mayonnaise, season with black pepper to taste and top with a slice of cheese. Assemble the sandwiches. You can eat them fresh or toast them to melt the cheese.

—

CIBIMEMO

* *If you can't get pecorino cheese, you can use another melting cheese such as provolone or cheddar.*

** *The key to making soft poached chicken is not to overboil it as it will become dry.*

Everyone loves tonkatsu (pork katsu), the Japanese version of schnitzel. They are thicker than your usual schnitzel, tossed in flour, dipped in egg, coated with rough Japanese panko breadcrumbs and deep fried.

These days, many of our Melbourne friends who go to Japan eat at a tonkatsu restaurant and love it. When spoken, 'katsu' sounds like the Japanese word for 'winning', so people often eat tonkatsu before big sporting events or exams for good luck, and just because it is a good excuse to indulge. I like using pork hire-niku (fillet) rather than ro-su (loin). Fillet katsu is tender and has less fat. I sometimes cut them into smaller pieces so our kids can eat them too.

KATSU SANDWICH with PICKLED FENNEL and CUCUMBER

MAKES 4 SANDWICHES

¼ medium Savoy cabbage

2 tablespoons chopped flat-leaf (Italian) parsley

300 g (10½ oz) pork fillet

100 g (3½ oz) plain (all-purpose) flour

1 egg

300 g (10½ oz) panko breadcrumbs

oil, for deep-frying

2 tablespoons dijon mustard

8 slices seeded sourdough

¼ telegraph (long) cucumber, sliced

60 ml (2 fl oz/¼ cup) Japanese tonkatsu* or worcestershire sauce

2 tablespoons Japanese mayonnaise

PICKLED FENNEL AND CUCUMBER

1 fennel, cut in half and finely sliced

¼ cucumber, sliced

60 ml Amazu (page 211)

1 Finely shred the cabbage and soak it in cold water for 5 minutes, which will make it nice and crunchy. Drain well, then combine it with the parsley and mix well.

2 To make the pickled fennel and cucumber, mix all of the ingredients together and let them marinate for at least 30 minutes.

3 Cut the pork into 40–50 g (1½–1¾ oz) pieces and season with salt and pepper.

4 Sprinkle the flour on a plate, lightly beat the egg in a small bowl and place the panko breadcrumbs on a second plate. To crumb the pork, dip the pieces into the flour, then into the egg, then coat them evenly with breadcrumbs.

5 Heat the oil in a deep-fryer or large, heavy-based saucepan (fill the pan to a depth of approx. 5 cm/2 in) until it reaches 170°C (340°F) when tested with a cooking thermometer. Deep-fry the pork for about 5 minutes, until crispy and light brown. Transfer the pieces to a wire rack with paper towel underneath to catch excess oil.

6 Spread the dijon mustard on 4 slices of sourdough. Arrange some cabbage on top of each, then 3–4 slices of cucumber and 2–3 pieces of pork. Dollop some tonkatsu sauce on top. Spread the mayonnaise on the last 4 slices of bread and assemble the sandwiches. Serve with the pickles on the side.

—

CIBIMEMO

* *Tonkatsu sauce is available from Japanese or Asian grocers, or from large supermarkets.*

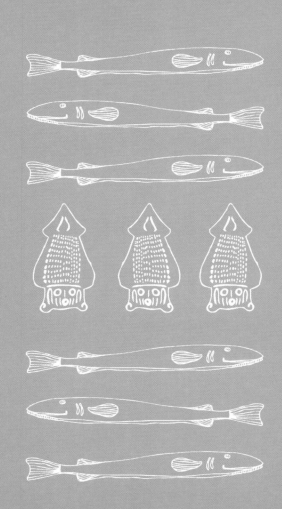

SEAFOOD

In Japanese cuisine, we eat fish a lot, both raw and cooked. The best way to eat fish (other than as fresh sashimi or sushi) is to simply salt and grill it yaki-sakana (grilled fish) style, like a fisherman on his boat, and eat it with a dash of soy sauce and a squeeze of lemon or yuzu. My seafood recipes are all easy to make, are full of tasty Japanese flavours and have some western twists that make each dish special.

White fish, fennel and miso go surprisingly well together. The sweetness of the roasted fennel fuses perfectly with the fish's flavour, while cream and miso give the dish a nice depth. It's simple to make, too: once you have prepared the white fish and fennel, all you do is bake everything together in an oven dish. This comforting east-meets-west gratin is perfect as a winter warmer. We call this dish 'my hot pan', as we usually cook and serve it in beautiful Japanese nanbu-tekki (cast-iron pans) as individual starters, but it can easily be made using small enamel trays or a larger baking dish.

WHITE FISH GRATIN with FENNEL and CHERRY TOMATOES

SERVES 4

1 large or 2 small fennel bulbs,
cut into thin wedges

75 ml (2½ fl oz) olive oil

400 g (14 oz) rockling, cod
or similar white fish

100 g (3½ oz) cornflour (cornstarch)

60 g (2 oz/1 cup) panko breadcrumbs

60 g (2 oz) parmesan cheese, grated

1 tablespoon chopped flat-leaf (Italian)
parsley

150 ml (5 fl oz/½ cup) thickened
(pouring/whipping) cream

90 ml (3 fl oz) Sweet Miso Sauce
(page 207)

180 g (6½ oz, about 12) vine tomatoes,
separated into bunches

1 Preheat the oven to 180°C (350°F). Grease the individual pans, enamel trays or one large baking dish (30×25 cm/12 in×10 in).

2 Arrange the fennel wedges in a roasting tin and roll them in 3 tablespoons of the oil and some salt and pepper. Roast for 20 minutes, or until the fennel turns soft.

3 Cut the fish into 3–4 cm (1¼–1½ in) cubes and season with salt and pepper. Sprinkle the cornflour on a plate and dip the fish in it, shaking off any excess.

4 Heat the remaining 2 tablespoons of oil in a frying pan and pan-fry the fish over a medium heat for a few minutes, until cooked through and light brown.

5 In a bowl, mix together the breadcrumbs, parmesan and parsley.

6 In the pans or baking dish or tray, arrange the fish and roasted fennel. Pour over the cream, drizzle over the miso sauce, and cover with the crumb mixture. Place the tomatoes on top, and bake for 10–15 minutes, or until the surface turns a nice light brown.

Everyone likes the battered, deep-fried beauty that is tempura. When I'm not working on the weekend and my family are all at home, I tend to cook it with soba or udon noodles – that's the Tanaka holiday lunch. I made this dish for our friend Mac Forbes's wine dinner, where it paired beautifully with his pinot noir.

Eating at a tempura restaurant in Japan is often exquisite and a bit fancy, but making tempura at home can be relaxed and casual. So don't stress too much: just enjoy the deep-fry. We use dashi and white soy sauce broth, which gives this dish an easy touch of elegance. Make sure you have some fresh vegetables to tempura as well, to add a seasonal touch to your meal.

FLATHEAD and CELERIAC TEMPURA with DASHI and WHITE SOY BROTH

SERVES 4

300–400 g (10½–14 oz) flathead fillets, cut at an angle into 10 cm (4 in) strips

200 g (7 oz/1⅓ cups) plain (all-purpose) flour

oil, for deep-frying

200 g (7 oz, about ¼) large celeriac, peeled and sliced into sticks

2 cauliflower florets, boiled and very thinly sliced

2 tablespoons finely chopped spring onion (scallion) to garnish

1 sheet (20 x 10 cm/8 x 4 in) dried nori (seaweed), crumbled, to garnish

¼ teaspoon sansho pepper* (or regular pepper)

DASHI AND WHITE SOY BROTH

1 tablespoon cornflour (cornstarch)

400 ml (13½ fl oz) Dashi (page 20)

3 tablespoons white soy sauce (see page 203)**

3 tablespoons mirin

½ tablespoon sake

½ tablespoon salt

1 To make the dashi broth, mix together 2 tablespoons water and the cornflour in a small bowl. In a large saucepan, bring the dashi to the boil. Add the soy sauce, mirin, sake and salt. Gently pour the cornflour mixture into the stock and stir until it thickens, about 2–3 minutes.

2 Season the flathead with salt and pepper.

3 In a bowl, whisk together the flour and 300 ml (10 fl oz) cold water until the flour crumbs disappear and the batter is smooth and runny.

4 Heat the oil in a deep-fryer or large, heavy-based saucepan (fill the pan to a depth of approx. 5 cm/2 in) until it reaches 170°C (340°F) when tested with a cooking thermometer. Meanwhile, mix the celeriac into the batter and coat well.

5 Using chopsticks, pick pieces of the celeriac out of the batter and gently put them into the deep-fryer or pan. Put as many pieces in as you can without overfilling; this step may have to be done in batches. Fry the celeriac for 3–5 minutes, or until crispy. Take the pieces out and transfer to a wire rack with paper towel underneath to catch the excess oil.

6 Coat the flathead in the batter, and deep-fry it for 3–5 minutes, or until crispy.

7 Reheat the broth if it has cooled, then divide it between four shallow serving bowls. Rest the flathead and celeriac tempura in the broth and gently arrange the cauliflower slices around it. Sprinkle over the spring onion, seaweed and sansho pepper.

—

CIBIMEMO

* Sansho pepper is a Japanese pepper often used for unagi (eel) and soba noodle soup. It has a nice lemony pepper flavour similar to Chinese sichuan pepper.

** Regular soy sauce works as well if you can't find white soy sauce.

When you write sawara (Spanish mackerel) in kanji (鰆), the characters within it are 魚 (fish) and 春 (spring), because the fish signifies the arrival of spring. We serve this dish on special occasions when we want to offer an intriguing twist on Japanese flavours at a Japanese-themed dinner. This way of preparing sawara is called saikyo-yaki style, where fish or meat is marinated with saikyo-miso (white miso), mirin and sake, then grilled. Our version is done with goma-miso (sesame miso), which gives the dish a nice roasted sesame flavour. We also use lime instead of the sudachi citrus* often used in Japan to add an extra zing at the end. This fish is best served with Perfect Stovetop Rice (page 18), Basic Miso Soup (page 20) and green vegetables.

SAWARA SAIKYO YAKI
with DAIKON and LIME

SERVES 4

400–500 g (14 oz–1 lb 2 oz) sawara (Spanish mackerel) fillet, cut into 4 pieces

150 g (5½ oz, about ¼) daikon (white radish), grated and excess liquid drained, to serve

4 lime wedges, to serve

SAIKYO-MISO WITH SESAME

1 tablespoon toasted white sesame seeds

100 g (3½ oz) white miso

3 tablespoons mirin

1 tablespoon sake

½ tablespoon maple syrup

1 To make the saikyo-miso, grind the toasted sesame seeds with a mortar and pestle. Add the white miso, mirin, sake and maple syrup and mix well.

2 Lay the fish pieces on a flat tray and coat both sides with the saikyo-miso mix. Let it marinate for at least 2 hours, or overnight, to really let the flavours infuse into the fish.

3 Preheat the grill (broiler) to 180°C (350°F).

4 Wipe the saikyo-miso marinade off the mackerel. Cook the fish under the grill for 3–5 minutes. Try not to overcook the fish or it will become very dry. If the meat is translucent and doesn't flake, it needs more time.

5 Serve the fish with the grated daikon and lime wedges.

—

CIBIMEMO

* Sudachi is a citrus fruit that comes from Japan's Shikoku Island. It is similar to lime, but has a stronger aroma and tanginess that complements grilled white fish and many soups. Use sudachi in this dish in place of lime, if you can find it.

I love carpaccio as much as I like sashimi. As long as the fish is fresh, I love to eat it raw: so good, and so Japanese. I love the simplicity of this authentic Italian recipe infused with Japanese flavours like ume (plum) dressing and layers of umami. We have very good kingfish in Australia, which makes this carpaccio a great dish if you want to impress your guests. It is simple, fresh and goes well with white wine or chilled sake.

KINGFISH CARPACCIO
with DASHI and UME

SERVES 4

200 g (7 oz) sashimi-grade kingfish fillet or similar, such as yellowtail or snapper

5 g (¼ oz/⅓ cup) tororo kombu (shaved and fluffy kombu)*

½ teaspoon soy sauce

2 tablespoons Ume (Plum) Dressing (page 211)

1 tablespoon snipped chives

micro herbs, to garnish

DASHI GELÉE

½ teaspoon powdered gelatine

200 ml (7 fl oz) Dashi (page 20)

1 teaspoon white soy sauce

1 To make the dashi gelée, dissolve the gelatine in 2 tablespoons water. In a saucepan, combine the dashi and the soy sauce and bring it to the boil. Add the gelatine mixture and stir until it has dissolved completely. Turn the heat off and pour the gelée into a shallow container. Once it has cooled down a bit, refrigerate the gelée for about 30 minutes, or until firm.

2 Using a sharp knife, thinly slice the kingfish into 5 mm (0.2 in) pieces. Refrigerate until you're ready to serve.

3 Arrange the tororo kombu on a flat serving plate, then arrange the kingfish slices on top. Lightly brush the fish with soy sauce.

4 Break the gelée up into crumbs with a fork and sprinkle over the fish, then pour the ume dressing evenly over the fish. Garnish with the chives and micro herbs.

—

CIBIMEMO

* *Tororo kombu is long, thin flakes of shaved kombu seaweed. It add lots of umami to this dish! Try to use the natural kind without any additives.*

If you cannot get tororo kombu, dashi or ume, you can make a simpler variation that's more like a classic Italian carpaccio. Just use yuzu juice and soy sauce in place of lemon juice and salt.

One of my favourite childhood dishes is buri-no-teriyaki (yellowfin teriyaki). During the Oshou-gatsu (New Year) period, my mum always grilled yellowfin teriyaki, and continues to do so today. Yellowfin is an iconic winter fish in Japan: we eat it to celebrate the season, and because it tastes so good. I use kingfish to make teriyaki instead of yellowtail – it is easier to get from the market and the flavour is lighter and subtler. I love this recipe's juiciness and richness, with lots of umami. If you feel like cooking an authentic Japanese dinner, serve this recipe with Perfect Stovetop Rice (Page 18), Miso Soup (Page 20) and some vegetables on the side.

KINGFISH TERIYAKI

SERVES 4

4 x 120 g (4½ oz) kingfish or yellowtail fillets

TERIYAKI-NO-TARE (TERIYAKI SAUCE)

2 tablespoons soy sauce

2 tablespoons sugar

2 tablespoons mirin

2 tablespoons sake

1 teaspoon fresh ginger, grated

1 Preheat the grill (broiler) to 170 °C (340 °F).

2 To make the teriyaki-no-tare, mix the ingredients together in a small bowl.

3 Arrange the fish on a flat tray. Pour over the teriyaki, coat the fish well and let it marinate for at least 30 minutes.

4 Grill (broil) the fish for 3–4 minutes, then flip and grill it for another 3–4 minutes, or until both sides are nice and brown. You can also prepare this dish by pan-frying the fish.

We often serve this classic salmon dish at CIBI. Meunière – a technique where fish is cooked in butter with lemon juice and parsley – is something we use a lot, adding some Japanese flavour. You really only need sweet tamari, lemon and a little bit of butter. This dish fits in well with both Japanese and western-style dinners and goes perfectly with any of the vegetable dishes from this book.

SALMON MEUNIÈRE with SWEET TAMARI and LEMON

SERVES 4

4 x 80–100 g (2¾–3½ oz) salmon fillets

80 g (2¾ oz) cornflour (cornstarch)

3 tablespoons olive oil

20 g (¾ oz) salted butter, finely chopped

lemon wedges, to serve

SWEET TAMARI SAUCE

1 tablespoon mirin

1 tablespoon sake

1 tablespoon sugar

1 tablespoon tamari

1 To make the sweet tamari sauce, combine the ingredients in a small bowl and mix well.

2 Season the salmon with some salt and pepper. Spread the cornflour on a plate and dip the fish in it to coat, shaking off any excess.

3 In a medium or large frying pan, heat the oil over a medium heat. Pan-fry the salmon for 3 minutes on each side, or until cooked through.

4 Turn off the heat and slowly pour in the sweet tamari sauce, completely coating the salmon. Add the butter and let it melt into the sauce. Spoon some of the sauce over the fish and serve it with the lemon wedges.

I like this recipe a lot. The daikon and yuzu ponzu help cut through the fattiness of the salmon, making the dish very refreshing and light. Serving pan-fried salmon with daikon and yuzu ponzu turns what could be a plain meal into a simple, very enjoyable Japanese dish. It goes well served with Early Autumn Salad (page 34) and Roasted Japanese Pumpkin (page 53).

PAN-FRIED SALMON with DAIKON and YUZU PONZU

SERVES 4

4 x 100–125 g (3½–4½ oz) salmon fillets

100 g (3½ oz) cornflour (cornstarch)

2 tablespoons olive oil

150 g (5½ oz, about ¼) daikon (white radish), grated, to garnish

2 tablespoons Yuzu Ponzu (page 208)*

1 teaspoon shichimi-togarashi (Japanese seven spice), to garnish

1 Season the salmon with salt and pepper. Sprinkle the cornflour on a plate and dip both sides of the fish in it to coat, shaking off any excess.

2 In a frying pan, heat the oil over a medium heat and pan-fry the salmon for 3 minutes, until both sides are browned and it is cooked through.

3 Plate the salmon and sprinkle some daikon on top. Drizzle over the yuzu ponzu, then sprinkle on the shichimi-togarashi.

—

CIBIMEMO

* *Yuzu ponzu is one of my favourite sauces, as it lends main dishes and dressings a beautiful citrus flavour. All you need to do is mix yuzu juice or fresh yuzu with soy sauce and vinegar. If you can't find yuzu, then lemon is a good substitute.*

I used to help my mum make this dish when I was little. We had no baking tray at home in those days, as baking wasn't so common. Instead, it was fun to wrap the fillets in individual pieces of foil, bake them one by one and serve them with a little cube of butter and a slice of lemon on top. My family considered it a very 'high-end' western dish, but I've added sweet miso sauce for an eastern touch. I bake the salmon with mushrooms, but you can use other vegetables such as fennel, zucchini, capsicum or tomato: whatever flavour combination you like!

BAKED SALMON with AUTUMN MUSHROOMS and SWEET MISO SAUCE

SERVES 4

½ leek, sliced into 5 mm (¼ in) pieces

1 medium onion, cut in half and thinly sliced

4 x 90–100 g (3–3½ oz) salmon fillets

3 tablespoons Sweet Miso Sauce (page 207)

8 thin lemon wheels

100 g (3½ oz) shimeji mushrooms*

50 g (1¾ oz) enoki mushrooms*

20 g (¾ oz) salted butter

1 tablespoon finely sliced spring onion (scallion), to garnish

juice of ½ lemon, to garnish

1   Preheat the oven to 200°C (400°F).

2   Cut out four 30 x 30 cm (12 x 12 in) squares of baking paper.

3   Divide the leek and onion between the four squares, then lay the salmon pieces on top. Pour the miso sauce over the salmon, then top with the lemon wheels, mushrooms and butter. Close each parcel, tying it together with kitchen string.

4   Transfer the parcels to a baking tray and bake for 15–20 minutes.

5   Plate the parcels, cut them open, then garnish with spring onion and lemon juice. Serve immediately.

—

CIBIMEMO

* *You can buy many different kinds of Japanese mushrooms: shimeji, enoki, eringi (king oyster), maitake (oyster), shiitake, etc. The texture and flavour of shimeji and enoki are great for this dish, but button or brown mushrooms are good substitutes if you can't find the former.*

This is a fun recipe to prepare with your family on a Sunday afternoon. Kids love to shape their own wontons. The crispy wonton and prawn texture is great. Adding shiso leaves gives the wontons an extra bit of refreshing flavour. Serving it with namasu (marinated daikon with cucumber) adds a nice, subtle touch.

CRISPY PRAWN WONTONS
with DAIKON NAMASU

20 WONTONS (SERVES 4–6)

20 wonton sheets

1 tablespoon cornflour (cornstarch)

20 king prawns (shrimp), peeled, tails on and heads removed

10 shiso leaves, halved (see page 202)

oil, for deep-frying

DAIKON NAMASU*

150 g (5½ oz, about ¼) daikon (white radish), finely sliced and cut into strips

¼ medium carrot, finely sliced and cut into strips

¼ telegraph (long) cucumber, finely sliced and cut into strips

2 tablespoons toasted black sesame seeds

60 ml (2 fl oz) Amazu (page 211)

1 To make the daikon namasu, combine all the ingredients in a bowl. Mix in the amazu and let the vegetables marinate for at least 30 minutes.

2 Lay a wonton sheet on a dry chopping board so that one corner is pointing towards you. Mix together the cornflour and 3 tablespoons water, then brush it on the sheet's edges – this is what will seal the wonton. Arrange a prawn and half a shiso leaf in the middle of the sheet, leaving the prawn's tail hanging over the corner facing you. Fold the top corner of the wonton sheet over, forming a triangle, and press down on the edges to seal. Fold the two top corners over a bit to form two tiny, dog-eared triangles – this will help the wonton stay sealed as it fries. Repeat with the rest of the wontons. You can fold them into any shape you like, really, so long as the filling is well-sealed on all sides!

3 Heat the oil in a deep-fryer or large, heavy-based saucepan (fill the pan to a depth of approx. 5 cm/2 in) until it reaches 170°C (340°F) when tested with a cooking thermometer. Deep-fry the wontons for a few minutes, or until they turn nice and brown.

4 Plate the wontons and serve them with the namasu on the side.

—

CIBIMEMO

* *Namasu is a lightly pickled vegetable salad where vinegar and sugar are used as the marinade, sometimes with the addition of yuzu peels or chillies. A typical namasu dish contains shredded daikon and carrot.*

I don't eat as much seafood as I used to in Japan, so I often feel like I need a boost of calcium and minerals. That is why I cook these easy school prawns. I simply toss them in cornflour spiced with ao-nori (green seaweed flakes) and prepare them as an isobe-age (seaside deep-fry). So crispy and tasty. This is one of those dishes that once you start eating it, you can't stop! It is great as an after-work snack paired with beer, white wine or sake.

SCHOOL PRAWNS ISOBE-AGE

SERVES 4

300 g (10½ oz) fresh or
frozen school prawns (shrimp)
(if frozen, thaw a day before
in the fridge)

100 ml (3½ fl oz) sake

1 teaspoon salt

200 g (7 oz) cornflour (cornstarch)*

1 tablespoon ao-nori
(green seaweed flakes)

oil, for deep-frying

lemon wedges, to serve

fresh chilli, finely sliced, to garnish
(optional)

1   In a bowl, combine the prawns with the sake, salt and some pepper to season, and let them marinate for 15–20 minutes minutes. Drain well.

2   In another bowl, mix together the cornflour and ao-nori. Coat the school prawns with the cornflour mix.

3   Heat the oil in a deep-fryer or large, heavy-based saucepan (fill the pan to a depth of approx. 5 cm/2 in) until it reaches 170°C (340°F) when tested with a cooking thermometer. Deep-fry the school prawns until they turn crispy and brown, about 3–5 minutes. Serve them with the lemon wedges and chilli, if you like.

—

CIBIMEMO

Isobe-age is a tempura or deep-fry done with ao-nori (seaweed flakes). This method is great when cooking with chikuwa (Japanese fish cake tubes), kakiage (shredded vegetables with small shrimp), sardines – basically with any kind of seafood.

This has become our signature summer dish at our food project space, Minanoie. What I like about it is how nicely it combines western tartare and eastern flavours: tuna sashimi tartare with yuzu pepper and a dash of soy sauce. Clean and refreshing, we add some vegetables to make it a layered and well-balanced dish. We serve this tartare with rice and a green leaf salad, but you can also serve it as a canapé on slices of crusty baguette.

CIBI TUNA TARTARE

SERVES 4

500 g (1 lb 2 oz) sashimi-grade tuna, cut into 1.5 cm (½ in) cubes

60 g (2 oz) cucumber, finely cubed

40 g (1½ oz, about 3) radishes, finely cubed

2 tablespoons small capers (in vinegar)

1 tablespoon caper juice

5 tablespoons snipped chives

2 avocados, cubed

juice of 1 lemon

75 ml (2½ fl oz) extra-virgin olive oil

1 quantity Perfect Stovetop Rice (page 18)

50 g (1¾ oz) mixed salad leaves

2 tablespoons Yuzu Pepper Mayo Dressing (page 211)

4 teaspoons soy sauce

2 sprigs chervil, finely chopped, to garnish

1 To make the tartare, combine the tuna, 4 tablespoons of the cucumber, 2 tablespoons of the radish, capers, caper juice, 3 tablespoons of the chives, avocado, lemon juice and 3 tablespoons of the oil in a bowl. Season with salt and pepper to taste.

2 Divide the rice between four serving bowls. Arrange some salad leaves on the rim of each.

3 Drizzle ½ tablespoon of the oil over each bowl of rice, then arrange some tuna tartare on top. Drizzle half a tablespoon of yuzu mayonnaise over the tartare in each bowl, then garnish with the remaining radish, cucumber and chives.

4 Drizzle 1 teaspoon of soy sauce over each bowl and garnish with chervil.

I like to eat this dish just when spring arrives. It is pink, a colour that reminds me of flowers blooming, and seared (not warm, not cold – just like spring). It's so easy, and the colour makes it very beautiful. You slice the tuna and serve it like a sashimi slice with carmelised red onions. Lightly brushing the tuna with soy sauce adds a Japanese touch that makes the dish complete. In summer, I use this as a taco filling and it is so good. The tuna goes well with Asparagus with Tofu and Lemon Miso (page 26) and Heirloom Carrots, Yellow and Green Beans with Yuzu Miso (page 83).

PAN-SEARED TUNA
with CARAMELISED ONIONS

SERVES 4

300 g (10½ oz) sashimi-grade tuna

50 g (1¾ oz) cornflour (cornstarch)

3 tablespoons olive oil

1 tablespoon soy sauce

CARAMELISED RED ONIONS*

1 tablespoon olive oil

1 red onion, cut in half
and thinly sliced

¼ teaspoon salt

1 tablespoon caster (superfine) sugar

3 tablespoons red-wine vinegar

1 To make the caramelised onions, heat the oil in a frying pan over a medium heat. Sauté the onions for 5–7 minutes, until they are translucent and soft. Add the salt and sugar and mix well, letting it cook for another few minutes. Add the vinegar and mix well. Turn off the heat.

2 Season the tuna with salt and pepper, then toss it lightly in the cornflour.

3 Heat the 3 tablespoons of oil in a frying pan over a medium–high heat. Once the pan is hot, sear the tuna for about 5 minutes on one side and 3 minutes on the other, but make sure not to overcook it – the tuna should be cooked on the outside and raw inside.

4 Let the tuna cool on a cutting board, then cut it into 1 cm (½ in) thick slices with a sharp knife (this is important, as using a dull knife will make the tuna become crumbly).

6 Plate the tuna slices. Brush them with the soy sauce and put some caramelised onions on top.

—

CIBIMEMO

* *Caramelised red onions are a versatile addition to many dishes. We use them in sandwiches and salads all the time, as well as in frittatas and on pizza. You can make a big batch and keep it in the refrigerator – they'll last for up to a week.*

I remember getting so excited when my mum made this dish with flounder – I would eat the whole fish by myself. She used to deep-fry the flounder first, then pan-fry it with delicious amazu-an (sweet and sour sauce; kake means 'to pour'). While any white fish goes well with this sauce, this recipe uses swordfish because it has more umami than other white fish. You don't need to deep-fry it – just pan-fry and mix it with the amazu-an. The addition of mushrooms makes it a great dish for autumn or winter. The swordfish goes well served with Roasted Jerusalem Artichokes (page 92) and Pickled Turnip, Apple, Beancurd and Mizuna Salad (page 98).

PAN-FRIED SWORDFISH
with AMAZU-ANKAKE

SERVES 4

50 g (1¾ oz) enoki mushrooms

4 x 100 g (3½ oz) swordfish fillets

125 ml (4 fl oz/½ cup) sake

3–4 cm (1¼–1½ in) piece of fresh ginger, grated

50 g (1¾ oz) cornflour (cornstarch)

3 tablespoons olive oil

1 tablespoon snipped chives, to garnish

AMAZU-AN

1 tablespoon cornflour (cornstarch)

135 ml (4½ fl oz) rice vinegar

3 tablespoons sake

3 tablespoons soy sauce

3 tablespoons sugar

1 To make the amazu-an, mix together the cornflour and 3 tablespoons water in a small bowl. Combine the rice vinegar, sake, soy sauce and sugar in a saucepan and bring it to the boil. Turn the heat down to low and pour in the cornflour mixture, gently stirring until the sauce thickens.

2 Drop the mushrooms into the amazu-an and let them cook for a couple of minutes.

3 Season the fish with salt and pepper. Combine the sake and ginger and pour it onto a flat tray. Coat both sides of the fish and let it marinate for 20–30 minutes.

4 Pour the cornflour onto a plate and coat both sides of the fish with it, brushing off any excess.

5 Heat the oil in a frying pan over a medium heat and pan-fry the fish for a few minutes, then flip and cook the other side for a few minutes (4–5 minutes total), or until it is nice and brown.

6 Pour the warm amazu-an over the fish to coat it well.

7 Plate the fish, then garnish each piece with chives.

When summer came, my mum used to make this dish for lunch with fresh, small sardines. Nanban means 'western-style' (particularly from southern Europe) and zuke means 'marinade'. I love how refreshing the sour flavours are on a hot summer's day. Eaten cold, this is a great dish for a balanced lunch or dinner in the middle of the hot season. This is also nice to serve warm after summer has passed. There is no need to be precise when measuring out your vegetables – just use as much of each as you like.

SARDINE NANBAN-ZUKE
with SUMMER VEGETABLES

SERVES 4

¼ yellow capsicum (bell pepper), finely cut into sticks

¼ red capsicum (bell pepper), finely cut into sticks

½ Lebanese (short) or ¼ telegraph (long) cucumber, finely cut into sticks

½ medium carrot, finely cut into sticks

150 ml (5 fl oz) Nanban Sauce (page 208)

8–10 small sardines, heads removed and gutted*

100 g (3½ oz) cornflour (cornstarch), for coating

oil, for deep-frying

1 Arrange the vegetables on a flat tray. Pour over the nanban sauce, mix well, and let them marinate for approximately 30 minutes.

2 Season the sardines with salt and pepper. Dip them in the cornflour to coat both sides.

3 Heat the oil in a deep-fryer or large, heavy-based saucepan (fill the pan to a depth of approx. 5 cm/2 in) until it reaches 170°C (340°F) when tested with a cooking thermometer. When the oil is hot, deep-fry the sardines until they are light brown and crispy, about 4–5 minutes.

4 Put the sardines on the tray with the vegetables and let them marinate for 5–10 minutes before serving.

—

CIBIMEMO

* We serve this dish with salmon at CIBI, pan-frying it instead of deep-frying. Using salmon can be simpler and easier than using sardines, which makes it perfect if you're in a hurry. If your sardines are small to medium in size and you deep-fry them for 7–8 minutes, you can enjoy them bones and all.

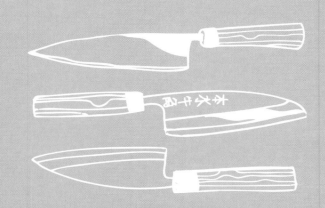

MEAT

In Japanese cooking, most meat dishes include vegetables. At CIBI, we like to do the same. All of our meat recipes have a vegetable component to ensure that they are healthy and interesting. Many complement the seasons, like our delicious summertime reviver Shabu-Shabu Salad. We hope you enjoy exploring these tasty, well-balanced recipes and that they add a special touch to your table.

This great chicken kara-age (deep-fried meat) dish is always one of the most popular choices when we serve it as our lunch special or at functions. People are often impressed by the flavour combination: kara-age and daikon-oroshi (grated daikon) – the freshness of the daikon beautifully balances the dish and cuts through the oil used in deep-frying. This mizore (a seasoning of grated daikon with soy and vinegar) is the kind of dish that once you start eating, it's hard to stop!

CHICKEN MIZORE-AE
with DAIKON and PONZU

SERVES 4

400 g (14 oz, about 3) boneless chicken thighs, cut into small pieces

100 ml (3½ fl oz) sake

2 cm (¾ in) piece of fresh ginger, grated

oil, for deep-frying

150 g (5½ oz) cornflour (cornstarch)*

150 g (5½ oz, about ¼) daikon (white radish), grated and excess liquid drained

90 ml (3 fl oz) Yuzu Ponzu (page 208)

1 tablespoon snipped chives, to garnish

¼ teaspoon shichimi-togarashi (Japanese seven spice), to garnish

1 Season the chicken with salt and pepper. In a bowl, combine it with the sake and ginger and let it marinate for 20–30 minutes.

2 Heat the oil in a deep-fryer or large, heavy-based saucepan (fill the pan to a depth of approx. 5 cm/2 in) until it reaches 170°C (340°F) when tested with a cooking thermometer.

3 Add the cornflour and chicken to a bowl and toss to coat. Deep-fry the chicken for 5 minutes, or until it turns crispy and brown. Transfer it to a wire rack with paper towel underneath to catch the excess oil.

4 In a bowl, mix together the daikon and the yuzu ponzu. (If the grated daikon seems a little wet, drain off any excess liquid before mixing it with the other ingredients). Toss in the fried chicken and let it marinate for 10–15 minutes. Sprinkle the chives and shichimi-togarashi on top.

—

CIBIMEMO

The flavours in this dish are also tasty with deep-fried eggplant, mushrooms and seafood.

* *Cornflour is often used in place of flour when pan-frying or deep-frying and to thicken broths or sauces. In Japanese cooking, we also use katakuri-ko (potato starch) to do the same job, but I prefer cornflour, especially for frying – the texture is crispy and crunchy.*

This is one of the great dishes my grandma and mum used to cook for our lunches or bento boxes. Traditionally, a soboro (which means 'crumbly') dish is a bowl of rice with a combination of minced chicken soboro, egg soboro and some greens. The minced chicken is usually cooked with soy, sugar and mirin, but we add red miso and lots of ginger to give it a kick of interesting and tasty flavours. We serve this dish with half-boiled eggs marinated in soy and kombu instead of egg soboro.

This dish is great for lunch or a quick, kid-friendly dinner. The best way to enjoy it is to use a spoon and fork to mix it all in so every bite becomes tasty and delicious. I recommend you make the soy eggs a day ahead so this dish is quick and simple.

CHICKEN SOBORO, SOY EGGS and GREENS with RICE

SERVES 4

1 tablespoon olive oil

500 g (1 lb 2 oz) minced (ground) chicken

3⅓ tablespoons red miso

4–5 cm (1½–2 in) piece of fresh ginger, grated

3⅓ tablespoons sugar

1½ tablespoons mirin

1 tablespoon sake

½ tablespoon soy sauce

1 tablespoon toasted white sesame seeds

1 quantity Perfect Stovetop Rice (page 18), to serve

100 g (3½ oz) green beans, trimmed, blanched and roughly chopped

100 g (3½ oz) frozen edamame, boiled and drained

mizuna salad or mixed salad leaves, to garnish

thinly sliced radish, to garnish

SOY EGGS

pinch of salt

4 eggs

60 ml (2 fl oz/¼ cup) tamari

1 tablespoon sugar

3 cm (1¼ in) piece of dried kombu seaweed, cut into long strips

Make the soy eggs

1 Bring a saucepan of water to the boil over a medium–high heat. Add the pinch of salt, then slowly drop the eggs in using tongs so as not to break them. Bring the water back to the boil, then reduce the heat to low and cook, uncovered, for 6 minutes (or, if you prefer a less runny yolk, 8 minutes). Once they're cooked, cool the eggs under cold running water.

2 In a separate saucepan, mix the tamari, sugar and kombu with 140 ml (4½ fl oz) water. Bring the mixture to the boil, then turn off the heat. While the sauce is heating up, peel the eggs.

3 When the sauce is cool, add the eggs and let them marinate for at least 2 hours.

Make the chicken soboro

1 Heat the oil in a large, shallow frying pan over a high heat. Add the chicken and fry until it is almost cooked.

2 Add the miso, ginger, sugar, mirin, sake and soy sauce and mix well. Fry for 5–10 minutes, until the chicken is cooked through, then add the sesame seeds.

3 Divide the rice between 4 serving bowls, then top each with the chicken soboro, green beans and edamame. Garnish with the soy eggs, cut in half, and some salad leaves and radish slices.

—

CIBIMEMO

You can do a lot of things with chicken soboro: stuff vegetables, enjoy it with noodles and pasta, or put it on toast with cheese. Soy eggs are versatile, too: they are great with our Cold Ramen Salad (page 108).

I call this tori-dango (minced chicken ball) soup a 'super soup': it's so wholesome and nutritious that you'll feel like you are feeding your body all sorts of good things. It contains many different flavours, yet they blend in really well to create one very tasty soup. When you're feeling a bit down or lacking energy, this soup is the perfect pick-me-up.

TORI-DANGO SOUP with SPINACH, HAKUSAI and MUSHROOMS

SERVES 4–6

2 litres (68 fl oz/8 cups) Dashi (page 20)

3 shiitake mushrooms, finely chopped

3 tablespoons soy sauce

1 teaspoon salt

2–3 hakusai (Chinese cabbage) leaves, chopped into 2–3 cm (¾–1¼ in) pieces

30 g (1 oz) dried harusame (vermicelli noodles), soaked in warm water

3 tablespoons cornflour (cornstarch)

250 g (9 oz) English spinach, blanched and chopped, to garnish

coriander (cilantro) leaves, to garnish

30 g (1 oz/¼ cup) spring onions (scallions), chopped, to garnish

1 teaspoon yuzu pepper paste*, to garnish

TORI-DANGO (MINCED CHICKEN BALLS)

500 g (1 lb 2 oz) minced (ground) chicken

3 shiitake mushrooms, finely sliced

4–5 cm (1½–2 in) piece of fresh ginger, grated

2 tablespoons chopped spring onion (scallion)

1 tablespoon cornflour (cornstarch)

1 tablespoon soy sauce

1 tablespoon sesame oil

1 egg

1 teaspoon salt

1 Mix the tori-dango ingredients together well. You can use wet hands to shape the balls, but the softness of this mixture means that using two spoons is more effective. Each ball should be about 30 g (1 oz).

2 Pour the dashi into a large stockpot. Add the mushrooms and bring to the boil. Once the mushrooms are soft, after about 5 minutes, add the soy sauce and salt, then reduce the heat to low. Using a spoon, carefully lower the chicken balls into the stock. Simmer for 10 minutes, until they are cooked. Add the hakusai and cook for 5 minutes. Add in the harusame and cook for a further 2 minutes.

3 In a small bowl, combine 60 ml (2 fl oz/¼ cup) water and cornflour and mix well. Add the cornflour mixture to the broth and stir until the soup is nice and thick.

4 Ladle the soup into bowls. Garnish with spinach, coriander and spring onion, then add the yuzu pepper paste on top.

—

CIBIMEMO

*   *You only need a tiny bit of yuzu pepper to enjoy its flavour and hint of spiciness. If you like spicy food, feel free to add some more. For kids, I recommend leaving it out, as it is very hot.*

Before we started CIBI, Zenta and I went on a long-dreamed-of trip to southern France. We walked around the town of Avignon and found a canteen cafe where locals were hanging out. After a warm greeting from the French mademoiselles, we ordered this delicious chicken dish served with barley. I have been thinking about it ever since.

When we opened Minanoie, I managed to recreate the dish. We serve it with brown rice and Beetroot and Daikon Salad (page 87). We have customers who come in and order it for lunch every day. We had a French customer who was so impressed by it that he said it made him feel like he was back home. This dish is not Japanese at all, but everyone loves it, and I'm happy to serve a classic French dish at CIBI. I like to share delicious food with everyone, no matter where it comes from. However, I do still make the brown rice with dried kombu seaweed to add a Japanese touch.

SLOW-COOKED CHICKEN with GREEN OLIVES

SERVES 4–6

1.2 kg (2 lb 10 oz, around 4–5) boneless, skinless chicken thighs or chicken leg quarters, cut into 5–6 cm (2–2½ in) pieces

120 g (4½ oz/about 1 cup) Sicilian green olives

3–4 garlic cloves, skin on

3–4 bay leaves, fresh or dried

4 parsley sprigs

2 thyme sprigs

300 ml (10 fl oz) olive oil

BROWN RICE*

450 g (1 lb) medium-grain brown rice

1½ tablespoons extra-virgin olive oil

5 x 5 cm (2 x 2 in) piece of dried kombu seaweed**

1 teaspoon salt

1　Soak the brown rice in water overnight, or for at least 6–8 hours.

2　Preheat the oven to 180°C (350°F).

3　Season the chicken with the salt and a few grinds of fresh pepper.

4　Add the chicken to a cast-iron stockpot or casserole dish with a heavy lid. Sprinkle over the olives, garlic, bay leaves, parsley and thyme. Pour over the olive oil.

5　Cover the chicken and bake for 1½ hours, or until the chicken is cooked through and the garlic is very soft.

6　While the chicken is cooking, drain the rice and put it in a saucepan or rice cooker. Cover with 540 ml (18 fl oz) water, add the extra-virgin olive oil, kombu and salt, and mix well.

7　Cover the rice and bring to the boil. Make sure not to remove the lid while it is cooking. Once steam starts escaping, reduce the heat to low. Let it cook for another 5 minutes, then turn the heat off and let it sit, covered, for at least 10 minutes.

8　Serve the chicken on a bed of rice. Spoon some of the oil from the stockpot on top – it goes really well with the rice.

—

CIBIMEMO

*　*You can serve this dish with barley or bread instead of brown rice. This brown rice recipe goes well with braised meat or fish too, and is especially good with Braised Koji Pork Belly (page 170).*

**　*If you cannot find dried kombu, don't worry. The dish is still delicious without it.*

This is one of my favourite and most easy-to-make recipes from my mum – pork cooked in black tea. When you cook pork in black tea, the tannins tenderise the meat and reduce the fat so it becomes light and clean. All you need to do is make strong black tea in a heavy pot, put the pork in and cook it. You'll also use the marinade to dress the salad so there is no waste – it is so simple, and so good. The leftover cold meat makes for a good summer lunch dish.

MUM'S PORK CHA-SHU

SERVES 4–6

2–3 black teabags (Ceylon or English Breakfast are nice)

500 g (1 lb 2 oz) pork shoulder or fillet

50 g (1¾ oz) mixed salad leaves

1 tablespoon finely sliced spring onion (scallion), to garnish

1 quantity Perfect Stovetop Rice, to serve (page 18)

CHA-SHU MARINADE*

100 ml (3½ fl oz) soy sauce

100 ml (3½ fl oz) mirin

3 tablespoons sake

3 tablespoons rice vinegar

1 In a large stockpot, bring 1 litre (34 fl oz/4 cups) water to the boil. Add the teabags and let them steep to make a very strong black tea.

2 Remove the teabags, transfer the pork to the stockpot and bring it to the boil. Turn the heat down to low and use a piece of baking paper to make an otoshi-buta (drop-lid). Cook the pork for about 40 minutes, until it is firm to the touch and its juices run clear when you pierce the meat with a knife.

3 While the pork is cooking, make the marinade. Combine all the ingredients in a saucepan and bring to the boil for 2 minutes. Cool the sauce and pour it into a rimmed tray or bowl.

4 Once the pork is cooked, remove it from the pot and coat it in the marinade. Let the pork cool.

5 To serve, arrange some salad leaves on each plate and dress with the leftover marinade. Thinly slice the pork and place it on the plate, and garnish with spring onion. Serve accompanied by rice. Leftover pork keeps in a tightly sealed container for up to 1 week*.

———

CIBIMEMO

* *This pork tastes even better after sitting for a day in the marinade, and goes well with Daikon and Mizuna Salad (page 76) and Heirloom Tomato Salad (page 40).*

I often cook this dish for our team dinners at CIBI. Everyone always goes back to the pot to help themselves to seconds and thirds. This is another great French recipe, but instead of using salt pork, I marinate the pork belly with koji (malted rice) and bay leaves a few days in advance. It has a nice balance of koji flavours on the nose and palate, and the meat is so amazingly tender. Adding shio-koji to this east-meets-west dish makes it the perfect balance between French and Japanese. It's great with red wine, but just as good with sake. Serve it with Brown Rice (page 164) and some greens or a salad.

BRAISED KOJI PORK BELLY
with TOMATOES and HERBS

SERVES 4–6

1 kg (2 lb 3 oz) pork belly*

6 bay leaves, fresh or dried

2 tablespoons olive oil

50 g (1¾ oz) salted butter

2 medium onions, thinly sliced

200 ml (7 fl oz) white wine

3–4 thyme sprigs

12–14 black peppercorns

3–4 garlic cloves, skin on

250 g (9 oz) cherry tomatoes

1 quantity Brown Rice (page 164), to serve

300 g (10½ oz) brussels sprouts, blanched, to serve

SHIO-KOJI**

250 g (9 oz) koji (malted rice) block

70 g (2½ oz) salt

1 To make the shio-koji, break up the koji and put it into a resealable container. Add the salt and mix well. Pour in 330 ml (11 fl oz) water and mix well. Seal the container and let it ferment at room temperature for about 1 week, stirring once a day, until the koji is nice and soft. (The time varies depending on the outside temperature. The fermentation process will be quicker in summer, so check regularly. The shio-koji is ready once the rice is soft to the touch). Once it's ready, keep the koji in the fridge. It will last for a couple of months.

2 Three to four days before cooking, marinate the pork belly. Cut little crosses all over the skin and rub 100 g (3½ oz) of the shio-koji into them. Combine the pork and 4 bay leaves in a large resealable plastic bag, and store in the fridge until you are ready to cook.

3 A few hours before cooking, take the pork out of the fridge and bring it to room temperature.

4 Preheat the oven to 180°C (350°F). Wipe the shio-koji and any excess liquid off the pork, making sure it is dry.

5 Heat the oil in a heavy cast-iron casserole dish over a medium–high heat. Once the oil is hot, add the pork belly and sear each side for 3–5 minutes, until brown.

6 Take the pork out of the casserole dish and lay it on a flat tray. Wipe the casserole dish with paper towel to remove any excess oil.

7 Add the butter and onion to the casserole dish and sauté over a low heat for 15–20 minutes, stirring occasionally, until the onions are caramelised. Turn the heat up to high and add the white wine, using a spatula to deglaze the pan. Cook off the wine for 3–5 minutes, then turn off the heat.

8 Add the pork belly to the onion, then add the thyme, remaining bay leaves, peppercorns and garlic. Pour 250 ml (8½ fl oz/1 cup) water over the pork. Cover and braise for 1–1.5 hours, until the pork is firm but springs back when touched.

9 Remove the lid and add the tomatoes. Continue braising the pork for 30 minutes. You can serve it straight away, but it also tastes great the day after. Serve with brown rice and blanched vegetables – brussels sprouts work well.

—

CIBIMEMO

*   *When you buy pork belly from your butcher, try to get thick pieces. They have a good amount of red meat in them as well as fat. Ask them to cut it into 8–10 cm (3¼–4 in) strips.*

** *You can buy shio-koji from a Japanese grocer, or buy koji and make your own shio-koji as we call for here. If you cannot get koji, you can substitute 2 tablespoons of salt for every 1 kg (2 lb 3 oz) of pork belly.*

You'll often see this classic Japanese pork dish on the menu at a teishoku-ya (Japanese lunch diner) as well as cooked at home. There are two ways to cook this dish – on the grill or in the pot. Our style is to cook it in a pot with vegetables, which makes the dish more balanced. It tastes better if you serve it with a bit of the sauce left in the bottom of the pot. Pair it with our Perfect Stovetop Rice (page 18) for a classic combination. It also goes well with our CIBI Coleslaw with Goma-Shio (page 66) or Hakusai, Kohlrabi and Mandarin Salad (page 67).

JAPANESE GINGER PORK

SERVES 4–6

800 g (1 lb 12 oz) sliced pork belly*

2 tablespoons olive oil

1–2 medium onions, thinly sliced

1 medium carrot, peeled and cut into thin strips

shichimi-togarashi (Japanese seven spice), to garnish

GINGER PORK MARINADE

4–5 cm (1½–2 in) piece of fresh ginger, grated

2 tablespoons chopped spring onion (scallion)

55 g (2 oz/¼ cup) sugar

3 tablespoons soy sauce

2 tablespoons mirin

½ teaspoon chilli flakes

1 To make the marinade, combine all the ingredients in a small bowl and mix well.

2 Cut the pork slices in half diagonally and cut off any excess fat. Marinate the pork in the sauce for 20–30 minutes.

3 Heat the oil in a heavy-based saucepan over a high heat. Sauté the onion and carrots for 5 minutes, until they become soft and the onion is translucent. Mix in the pork and the marinade. Cook until the pork turns light brown, then cover and simmer over a low heat for 15–20 minutes, or until the pork is cooked and the vegetables are soft.

4 Sprinkle a pinch of shichimi-togarashi on top and serve.

—

CIBIMEMO

*   *It may be hard to find the right thinness of sliced pork belly at your butcher or supermarket. You can ask your butcher to slice it as thinly as possible or you can slice it yourself. Otherwise, you can get frozen thin-sliced pork belly from most Asian grocers.*

This barbecue miso sauce recipe comes from my aunt. My parents and their sisters and brothers are very close, and they all live in the same region in Okayama. Retired and with their kids grown up, they often catch up and eat together. I happened to be there once when my aunt brought her sauce over for a barbecue. It was so tasty that I had to ask her for the recipe. At CIBI, we make all our sauces in house – I feel you just can't beat home-made sauce. Every time I do Japanese-style yaki-niku (barbecue) at home, I marinate the meat in this sauce for at least 30 minutes. That's the secret to barbecue success. You can try other meats or seafood, or even vegetables, instead of wagyu beef.

BARBECUE WAGYU BEEF
with MISO MARINADE

SERVES 4

400 g (14 oz) wagyu beef sirloin, cut to your preferred size

3–4 tablespoons Barbecue Miso Sauce (page 207)

1 Marinate the beef in the barbecue sauce for at least 30 minutes.

2 Heat the barbecue to hot and grill the beef until cooked to your liking.

3 Serve with extra barbecue sauce on the side.

—

CIBIMEMO

The beef goes well with a tomato-based side (see the recipes on pages 36, 39 and 40), or Crunchy Vegetable Salad with Black Sesame and Ginger (page 29).

In summer, our bodies get tired. We've all had those hot days when we don't feel like eating much. In Japan we have a word for it: natsu-bate, which roughly translates as 'worn out by summer'. To avoid natsu-bate, it's always good to eat the right foods – lots of seasonal and colourful vegetables alongside good quantities of meat or fish. In summer, we always serve dishes like this finely sliced beef cooked in broth and vegetables with sweet sesame dressing to help customers recover from natsu-bate!

Shabu-shabu, which translates to something like 'swish, swish', is a Japanese dish where thinly sliced beef is cooked briefly in simmering broth at the table. Once you make the shabu-shabu, mix it with vegetables and goma-dare and eat it as a wholesome salad.

SHABU-SHABU SALAD

SERVES 4

5 x 5 cm (2 x 2 in) piece of dried kombu seaweed

300–400 g (10½–14 oz) finely sliced beef*

130 ml (4½ fl oz) Goma-dare (Sesame Dressing) (page 208)

150 g (5½ oz, about ¼) daikon (white radish), cut into thin strips, to garnish

100 g (3½ oz) beetroot, cut into thin strips, to garnish

50 g (1¾ oz) mixed salad leaves, to serve

1 tablespoon snipped chives, to garnish

1   In a saucepan, soak the kombu in 1 litre (34 fl oz/4 cups) water. Bring it to the boil, then add the beef and cook for about 2 minutes, or until the meat changes colour**. Remove the beef and leave it to cool.

2   Dip the beef in the goma-dare (sesame dressing) to coat. Plate and garnish it with the daikon and beetroot, and serve the salad leaves on the side. Drizzle over some extra dressing and sprinkle the chives over the top.

—

CIBIMEMO

*   You may not be able to source finely sliced beef at your butcher, but you will find it at an Asian grocer – the meat is often sliced and sold frozen and its thinness is perfect for this dish. You can also make this recipe with sliced pork instead of beef.

** With shabu-shabu, you never want to cook the meat too long as it will get tough and hard. Just lightly cook it so the meat is tender.

This is one of my most unforgettable dishes. When I was working as a wine importer in Tokyo, I had a special dinner with international winemakers at a small bistro restaurant in Roppongi owned by an acclaimed sommelier. We were served a beautiful beef cheek stew, made extraordinary by a hint of hatcho (very dark) miso. At that time, there weren't many chefs using Japanese ingredients in French cuisine, and it was a perfect dish. To top it off, it worked superbly with Australian shiraz. I still remember the first mouthful and how amazing it was.

SLOW-COOKED BEEF CHEEK
with RED WINE and HATCHO MISO

SERVES 4

3 tablespoons olive oil

1 kg (2 lb 3 oz) beef cheek, fatty membranes trimmed off, cut into 5–7 cm (2–2¾ in) pieces

1 large onion, finely chopped

1 garlic clove, sliced

1 medium carrot, finely chopped

1 celery stalk, finely chopped

1 tablespoon tomato paste (concentrated purée)

2 tablespoons plain (all-purpose) flour

1 litre (34 fl oz/4 cups) red wine

2–3 bay leaves, fresh or dried

2–3 thyme sprigs

2 tablespoons hatcho (very dark) miso

2 tablespoons thickened (pouring/whipping) cream, to serve

1 tablespoon chopped flat-leaf (Italian) parsley, to serve

steamed vegetables, to serve (optional)*

1 Preheat the oven to 150°C (300°F).

2 Heat 2 tablespoons of the oil in a large cast-iron stockpot over a high heat. Sear the beef cheek on each side for 3–5 minutes, until nicely browned. Put the beef cheek on a plate and loosely cover it with foil to keep warm.

3 Reduce the heat to medium–high and add the remaining tablespoon of oil. Sauté the onion and garlic for 5 minutes, or until the onion is translucent. Add the carrot and celery and sauté for another 5 minutes, until soft.

4 Return the beef and its juices to the pot and stir well. Season with salt and pepper, then add the tomato paste and stir well. Sprinkle the flour evenly over the beef and stir it in.

5 Pour the wine into a separate saucepan and bring it to the boil. Boil for 5 minutes to cook off the alcohol.

6 Pour the wine in with the beef and simmer over a high heat for about 5 minutes, stirring occasionally, until the liquid thickens. Add the bay leaves and thyme, and check and adjust the seasoning if necessary.

7 Make an otoshi-buta (drop lid) out of baking paper and place it on top of the ingredients in the pot. Put the pot in the oven and cook for 1½ hours. Add the hatcho miso and stir gently, then cook for another 30 minutes, until the beef is very tender.

8 Finish each bowl of stew with a little cream and some parsley. The beef is even more enjoyable if you let it sit overnight and eat it the next day.

—

CIBIMEMO

* *This dish is nice eaten with vegetables. We often steam small ones like potatoes, Dutch carrots, onions and turnips.*

This is a very authentic Japanese beef recipe. Shigureni is a kind of tsukudani (preserved dish cooked with sugar and soy sauce). If you can get thinly sliced beef from your butcher or Asian grocery store, it is perfect. If you can't, you can use beef strips instead. People often eat it as a gyu-don (beef rice bowl) with raw egg, but at CIBI we serve it on iceberg lettuce leaves. It makes a great party snack.

BEEF SHIGURENI
with ICEBERG LETTUCE

SERVES 4

2 tablespoons olive oil

300 g (10½ oz) sliced beef or beef strips, finely sliced

2 tablespoons soy sauce

2 tablespoons mirin

1 tablespoon sugar

1 tablespoon sake

3 cm (1¼ in) piece of fresh ginger, grated

150 g (5½ oz, about ¼ head) iceberg lettuce, leaves cut into squares

2 tablespoons Japanese mayonnaise

2 tablespoons snipped chives, to garnish

1 tablespoon toasted white sesame seeds, to garnish

1 teaspoon shichimi-togarashi (Japanese seven spice), to garnish

ito-togarashi (angel hair chilli, see CIBI Memo on page 117), to garnish (optional)

1   Heat the oil in a saucepan over a medium–high heat. Add the beef and stir-fry until it changes colour, about 5 minutes. Add the soy sauce, mirin, sugar, sake and ginger and stir well. Cook until the liquid has almost disappeared, skimming off any foam that rises to the surface.

2   Set out the iceberg leaves, which will serve as small plates. Brush a little mayonnaise onto each leaf. Put some beef on each leaf, then sprinkle with chives, sesame seeds, shichimi and ito-togarashi (if using).

—

CIBI MEMO

If you want a quick and hearty lunch dish, make this into a gyu-don (beef rice bowl). Put rice in a bowl and place the shigureni on top. I recommend eating it with some vegetables or a green salad.

SWEETS

At CIBI, we prefer our sweets not to be too sugary. That way, you can enjoy the wonderful flavours of the core ingredients. It's a special joy to share these recipes, which have become firm favourites with our customers over the years. They are simple, tasty, and include some classic Japanese touches that make them a unique and special treat. Enjoy!

At CIBI, we love infusing western dishes with Japanese flavours, like in this classic Italian dessert. I always cook this panna cotta for our team dinners and Japanese-themed events. Creamy and very soft, it makes a great after-dinner treat or can be enjoyed for afternoon tea. I make it in two different flavours: ginger and sesame, and both taste quite Japanese. Our desserts are never overly sweet, so adding kuro-mitsu (brown sugar syrup) gives it a nice, sweet depth that complements the sesame and ginger.

SESAME and GINGER PANNA COTTA

EACH RECIPE MAKES 4–5

SESAME PANNA COTTA

1½ teaspoons gelatine

350 ml (12 fl oz) full-cream (whole) milk

150 ml (5 fl oz) thickened (pouring/whipping) cream

40 g (1½ oz) unhulled tahini

40 g (1½ oz) caster (superfine) sugar

toasted white sesame seeds, to garnish

GINGER PANNA COTTA

1½ teaspoons gelatine

350 ml (12 fl oz) full-cream (whole) milk

3–4 cm (1¼–1½ in) piece of fresh ginger, finely sliced

½ vanilla bean, split lengthways and seeds scraped

40 g (1½ oz) caster (superfine) sugar

190 ml (6½ oz) thickened (pouring/whipping) cream

KURO-MITSU (BROWN SUGAR SYRUP)

50 g (1¾ oz) brown sugar

Make the sesame panna cotta

1 In a small bowl, combine the gelatine with 2 tablespoons water and mix well.

2 Combine the milk, cream, tahini and sugar in a saucepan over a medium heat, and bring to the boil, stirring occasionally, until the tahini is incorporated. Remove the saucepan from the heat. Add the gelatine mixture, stirring until well incorporated.

3 Strain the mixture through a fine-mesh sieve into a heatproof bowl.

4 Prepare a separate bowl of iced water. Float the bowl of panna cotta mixture in the iced-water, stirring for 10 minutes, or until it starts to thicken (the time will vary depending on how cold your iced-water bath is).

5 Pour the panna cotta into small serving bowls or containers* and refrigerate for at least 1 hour, or until firm. Their surfaces should move like soft jelly when you shake them gently.

6 Before serving, drizzle kuro-mitsu (see opposite page) over the top and sprinkle with toasted sesame seeds.

Make the ginger panna cotta

1 In a small bowl, combine the gelatine with 2 tablespoons water and mix well.

2 Combine the milk, ginger and vanilla in a saucepan. Cover and simmer over a low heat for about 5 minutes, then mash it with a spatula. Turn off the heat and let the mixture sit, covered, for 10 minutes. This will give the ginger time to infuse.

3 Add the gelatine mixture to the saucepan, stirring until well incorporated. Whisk in the sugar.

4 Strain the panna cotta through a fine-mesh sieve into a heatproof bowl, squeezing the ginger to get all of the juices out. Add the cream to the bowl and stir well.

5 Prepare a separate bowl of iced water. Float the bowl of panna cotta in the iced-water, stirring for 10 minutes, or until it starts to thicken, (the time will vary depending on how cold your iced-water bath is).

6 Pour the panna cotta into small serving bowls or containers* and refrigerate for at least 1 hour, or until firm. Their surfaces should move like soft jelly when you shake them gently.

7 Drizzle the kuro-mitsu (see opposite page) over the panna cotta before serving.

Make the kuro-mitsu

1 In a saucepan, combine the brown sugar and 100 ml (3½ oz) water, stirring until the sugar has dissolved. Bring to the boil, then reduce the heat to low and let it simmer for about 5 minutes. Turn off the heat and let the syrup cool**.

—

CIBIMEMO

* *Our panna cotta is very soft, so letting it set in individual cups makes it easy to divide up and serve. We like to use shallow teacups.*

** *Leftover syrup will keep in the fridge for several weeks and is great in iced coffee or with vanilla ice cream.*

We have served these muffins at CIBI every weekend since we opened. Two classic Japanese sweet ingredients – matcha (green tea) powder and sweet azuki beans – give these muffins their distinct flavour and the unique green colour that has caught the eye of many of our customers. Over the years, they have become the finishing note of our leisurely Japanese weekend breakfast experience (see page 16). They are great with both green tea and coffee.

GREEN TEA MUFFINS
with SWEET AZUKI BEANS

MAKES 6 MUFFINS

50 g (1¾ oz) unsalted butter, plus extra for greasing

80 g (2¾ oz) caster (superfine) sugar

1 egg

80 ml (2½ fl oz, ⅓ cup) full-cream (whole) milk

135 g (5 oz) plain (all-purpose) flour

3 tablespoons matcha (green tea) powder

2 teaspoons baking powder

120 g (4½ oz) sweet azuki bean paste*

flaked almonds, to garnish

1 Preheat the oven to 180°C (350°F). Grease a six-cup muffin tin with butter.

2 Melt the butter in a microwave or using a hot water bath (the aim is to melt it, not cook it). Set it aside to cool slightly.

3 In the bowl of a stand mixer, combine the sugar and egg and beat at high speed until the mixture is smooth and pale, about 3–5 minutes.

4 Add the melted butter and beat until well incorporated. Pour in the milk and beat again for 30 seconds to 1 minute.

5 Sift the flour, matcha and baking powder into the mixture, then stir with a spatula until smooth and shiny.

6 Pour the batter into the muffin tin, half-filling each cup. Add 2 tablespoons of azuki paste to the middle of each muffin. Divide the remaining batter between the cups, pouring in just enough to cover the filling.

7 Sprinkle almond flakes on top of each muffin and bake for 20–25 minutes, until they are nice and fluffy and a skewer inserted in the middle of a muffin comes out clean. Aim to take them out of the oven just before they start to turn golden brown. Allow to cool before serving.

—

CIBIMEMO

* If you cannot find sweet azuki bean paste, you can use 50 g (1¾ oz) of couverture white chocolate.

This is my simplest, easiest fruit salad, and an easy way to impress your friends. Just a little bit of orange blossom water and maple syrup gives the berries a magical flavour – it will feel like you are eating dessert at a nice restaurant. It is great with ice cream, chocolate cake, tarts, mousse, baked puddings and cheesecake. And, of course, you can serve it as is for breakfast, or as a healthy snack. It tastes best when freshly made, so I always mix everything together just before serving.

BERRY SALAD with ORANGE BLOSSOM and MAPLE SYRUP

SERVES 4

250 g (9 oz) strawberries, hulled and quartered

125 g (4½ oz/1 cup) raspberries

125 g (4½ oz) blueberries

handful of mint leaves

2 tablespoons maple syrup

¼ teaspoon orange blossom water

1   Wash the berries and dry them well with paper towel.

2   In a bowl, mix the berries and mint leaves. Pour in the maple syrup and orange blossom water and mix gently.

—

CIBIMEMO

This mixture of orange blossom water and maple syrup is also great with stonefruits, grapes, pears, oranges and apples.

Living in Australia means we get many kinds of beautiful seasonal fruit. I add lots of different fruits to this simple crumble to create a wholesome, balanced dish full of the flavours of the season. This fruit mix is the one we use most often, but you can easily adjust the fruits and spices to suit your taste.

Our kids love this crumble. None of these fruits are overly sweet, so I never feel guilty about serving it after dinner on the weekend. It can be served with ice cream if you want to treat yourself, or I like to add a dollop of fresh yoghurt.

SEASONAL FRUIT CRUMBLE

SERVES 4–6

3 tablespoons sultanas
(golden raisins)

5 dried apricots, finely chopped

150 g (5½ oz) sour cream

35 g (1¼ oz) caster (superfine) sugar

1 egg

¼ vanilla bean, split lengthways
and seeds scraped

1 apple or pear, cubed

zest and flesh of ½ orange, flesh cut
into 1–2 cm (½–¾ in) cubes

1–2 rhubarb stalks,
cut into 1–2 cm (½– ¾ in) cubes

100 g (3½ oz) fresh
or frozen raspberries

CRUMBLE TOPPING

75 g (2¾ oz) almond meal

150 g (5½ oz/1 cup) plain
(all-purpose) flour

150 g (5½ oz) caster (superfine) sugar

150 g (5½ oz) unsalted cold butter,
cubed

1   In a small bowl, soak the sultanas and apricots in enough warm water to cover them for at least 30 minutes, until nice and soft.

2   Preheat the oven to 180°C (350°F). Lightly grease a shallow 1.2 litre (41 fl oz) ovenproof dish, about 30 x 20 cm (12 x 8 in).

3   To make the crumble topping, combine the almond meal, flour and sugar.

4   To a large bowl, add the cold butter and sift in the flour mixture. Use your fingers to mix everything together until the mixture resembles pea-sized crumbles.

5   In a separate bowl, whisk together the sour cream, 35 g (1¼ oz) sugar, egg and vanilla seeds.

6   Drain the sultanas and apricots and add them to a bowl with the apple, orange zest and flesh, rhubarb and raspberries. Carefully pour the cream mixture in with the fruit and mix gently, then pour into the ovenproof dish.

7   Spread the crumble topping evenly over the fruit and bake for 20–30 minutes, or until the crumble is nice and brown.

These chocolate truffles are one of my favourite treats, and very easy to make. We always serve these petite sweets at the very end of our dinners, infusing them with Japanese or classic flavours depending on the evening's theme. These truffles are soft and smooth in texture, so it's best to keep them in the fridge until you are ready to serve. They are the perfect petit four with espresso or a strong green tea like gyokuro or matcha.

SAKE and MATCHA CHOCOLATE TRUFFLES

MAKES 20–24 TRUFFLES

SAKE TRUFFLES

3 dried prunes

3 tablespoons sake

135 g (5 oz) couverture milk chocolate*, finely chopped

25 g (1 oz) couverture dark chocolate (70% cocoa solids)*, finely chopped

85 ml (2¾ fl oz) thickened (pouring/whipping) cream

10 g (¼ oz) unsalted butter, softened

2 tablespoons cocoa powder, for dusting

MATCHA TRUFFLES

200 g (7 oz) couverture white chocolate*, finely chopped

100 ml (3½ fl oz) thickened (pouring/whipping) cream

10 g (¼ oz) unsalted butter, softened

25 g (1 oz) matcha powder, sifted

Make the sake truffles

1 Soak the prunes in the sake for at least 6–8 hours, or overnight. They will absorb the sake and become very soft. Drain the prunes and place on a paper towel to absorb excess liquid.

2 Grease a 15 x 15 cm (6 x 6 in) flat, shallow-sided container and line it with baking paper.

3 Combine the milk and dark chocolate in a heatproof bowl and set aside.

4 Heat the cream in a small saucepan over a medium–low heat. Turn off the heat just before it starts to boil.

5 Pour the hot cream over the chocolate and whisk until melted and smooth. If the chocolate doesn't melt completely, use a double boiler or put the bowl over a saucepan of simmering water until melted. Add the butter and whisk until melted and smooth.

6 Cut the prunes into 6–8 pieces. Mix them gently into the chocolate.

7 Pour the chocolate into the container and refrigerate for 2–3 hours, or until set. Once set, turn it out onto a chopping board. Cut it into 10–12 pieces, then roll each into a ball with your hands.

8 Arrange the truffles in the container and refrigerate again until set, for at least 30 minutes. Roll the balls in the cocoa powder just before serving.

Make the matcha truffles

1 While the sake and prune truffles are setting, grease a 15 x 15 cm (6 x 6 in) flat, shallow-sided container and line it with baking paper.

2 Put the chocolate in a heatproof bowl and set aside.

3 Heat the cream in a small saucepan over a medium–low heat. Turn off the heat just before it starts to boil.

4 Pour the hot cream over the chocolate and whisk until melted and smooth. If the chocolate doesn't melt completely, put it in a double boiler or place the bowl over a saucepan of simmering water until melted. Add the butter and whisk until melted and smooth.

5 Mix 4 teaspoons of matcha powder into the chocolate mixture until all combined.

6 Pour the chocolate into the container and refrigerate for 2–3 hours, or until set. Once set, turn it out onto a chopping board. Cut it into 10–12 pieces, then roll each into a ball with your hands.

7 Arrange the truffles in the container and refrigerate again until set, for at least 30 minutes. Roll the balls in the remaining matcha powder just before serving.

—

CIBIMEMO

* *Make sure to get couverture chocolate, which has a higher concentration of cocoa butter than other chocolates.*

This cake is one of our most popular sweets at CIBI. I was not planning to include it here, as it requires a bit of technique, but when our customers found out that we were writing a cookbook, we received many requests to include this popular cake. Making the right meringue, baking at the right temperature and giving it the right amount of baking time are all very important – they are the keys to success with this soft, moist gâteau.

GÂTEAU AU CHOCOLAT with RASPBERRIES

SERVES 6–8

140 g (5 oz) unsalted butter, plus extra for greasing

160 g (5½ oz) couverture dark chocolate (70% cocoa solids), finely chopped

20 g (¾ oz) couverture milk chocolate, finely chopped

3 eggs, separated

120 g (4½ oz) caster (superfine) sugar

2 tablespoons plain (all-purpose) flour

120 g (4½ oz) fresh or frozen raspberries

unsweetened (Dutch) cocoa powder, for dusting

1   Preheat the oven to 170°C (340°). Grease a 20 cm (8 in) round cake tin with butter. Trace around the bottom of the tin on a piece of baking paper. Cut out the circle and nestle it neatly in the tin.

2   Melt the butter and chocolate together in a double boiler or mix it in a heatproof bowl, over a saucepan of simmering water and stir until melted. Mix well, until the mixture is shiny, and take it off the heat.

3   Using an electric mixer, beat the egg whites for 2–3 minutes, until soft peaks form. Add 70 g (2½ oz) of the sugar and continue beating for 5–8 minutes, until the meringue is smooth and has formed stiff peaks.

4   Mix the remaining 50 g (1¾ oz) of sugar into the chocolate mixture, whisking lightly. Add the egg yolks and mix lightly. Sift in the flour and mix well. Add in one-third of the meringue and mix well. Fold in the rest of the meringue until completely combined. Add the raspberries and mix lightly once more.

5   Pour the mixture into the cake tin and smooth it out with a spatula or knife. Bake for 35–40 minutes. When the surface of the cake no longer jiggles when shaken and is dry to the touch, it is ready.

6   Dust the cake with cocoa powder before serving.

This is another CIBI customer favourite. Fig and ginger make for a great combination: the spiciness of the ginger complements the sweetness of the fig for a cake that is not overly sweet and very balanced, which we like. It's quite a traditional tea cake recipe, and perfect in cold weather. You will look forward to afternoon tea with this yummy cake. Try it with black tea, green tea or coffee. Sealed well, it can be stored in a cool place for a week.

FIG and GINGER CAKE

MAKES 1 CAKE

5 dried figs, stems removed and quartered

125 g (4½ oz) plain (all-purpose) flour

25 g (1 oz/¼ cup) almond meal

1 teaspoon baking powder

150 g (5½ oz) unsalted butter, at room temperature, plus extra, for greasing

125 g (4½ oz) caster (superfine) sugar

2 eggs, lightly beaten

70 g (2½ oz) ginger pieces from the Ginger Syrup, finely chopped, see below

½ tablespoon honey

1 tablespoon dark rum

GINGER SYRUP*

200 g (7 oz) caster (superfine) sugar

200 g (7 oz) fresh ginger, peeled and finely chopped

Make the ginger syrup

1 Cut a piece of baking paper to match the size of a large, heavy saucepan's lid. Make a little hole in the middle, forming a otoshi-buta (drop lid).

2 Combine the sugar and 400 ml (13½ fl oz) water in a large saucepan and simmer over a high heat until the sugar has dissolved. Add the ginger. Place the drop lid on the surface of the liquid. Bring it to the boil over a high heat, then turn the heat down to low and let it simmer for 20–30 minutes.

3 Once the syrup has cooled, store it in a sterilised glass jar and in a cool place or the refrigerator. It keeps for up to 3 months.

Make the cake

1 Preheat the oven to 175°C (350°F) and grease a 21 cm (8¼ in) loaf (bar) tin.

2 In a small bowl, cover the figs with warm water. Let them soak for 30 minutes, or until they turn soft, then drain. If you are in a hurry, use hot water and soak them for at least 10–15 minutes.

3 Sift the flour, almond meal and baking powder into a bowl.

4 Beat the butter and sugar in a bowl until pale and fluffy (5–8 minutes if beating by hand, 3–5 minutes if using an electric mixer). Add the eggs, one at a time, beating well after each addition.

5 Sift in the flour mixture and fold it in with a spatula. Once the flour is well incorporated, fold in the figs and ginger.

6 Pour the batter into the tin and bake for 40 minutes, or until a skewer inserted in the middle of the cake comes out clean.

7 While the cake bakes, combine the honey and rum in a small bowl and mix well.

8 Take the cake out of the oven. While the cake is still hot, brush the honey-rum mixture over the top. Allow the cake to cool before you serve it.

*   *We use this ginger syrup to make our lemon ginger tea. It's a great drink to warm you up and perfect if you are feeling sick. To make your own ginger tea, mix 2 tablespoons of syrup with some honey and a squeeze of lemon in a cup of hot water. In summer, you can also use the syrup to make ginger ale.*

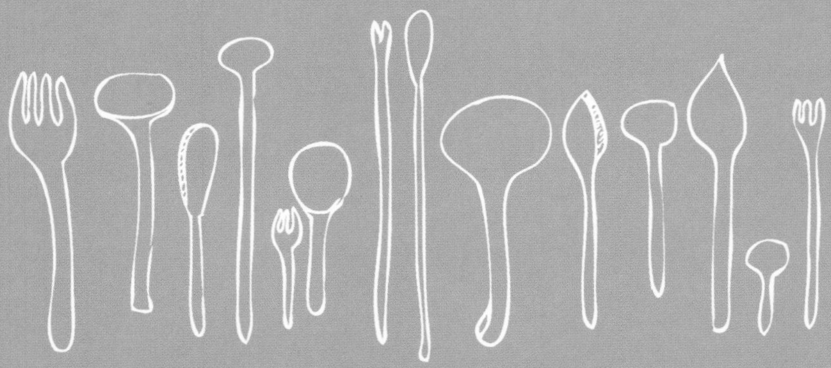

CIBI ESSENTIALS

Our love of food starts with quality produce, and our philosophy finds its simplest expression in our core ingredients and basic sauces, which provide a quick and easy way to add a touch of flavour to your favourite dishes or leftovers.

The cooking tools we use breathe life into our philosophy: the simplicity of their design, their functionality, and the attention to detail in their production make them a work of art, yet suited to everyday use. Handled with the love and care with which they were crafted, they add pleasure to the enjoyment of cooking, last for years and appeal to the cibi in all of us.

IN OUR KITCHEN

Whether you're cooking classic Japanese cuisine or our homely CIBI-style dishes, these core ingredients are a big part of what makes Japanese cooking so distinctive. We always have these in our pantry. They provide the basic flavours, textures and colours in our meals, along with the goodness to keep your body happy.

AO-NORI
A flaky, dry green seaweed often served on top of rice with toasted sesame seeds. Great for garnishing rice, tempura, okonomi-yaki (Japanese pancake), tako-yaki (octopus balls) and yaki-soba (Japanese stir-fried noodles).

AZUKI BEANS AND PASTE
We cook these beans with rice in winter in a dish called o-seki-han, as the beans lend it a beautiful red colour and nice texture. We serve it when we have something special to celebrate in Japan, as the colour red has long been associated with good luck. Of course, it is also very nutritious.

Azuki beans cooked with sugar form a thick, sweet paste that provides the sweet centre of many Japanese desserts. You can often find ready-made sweet azuki bean paste in tins or packets at Japanese or large Asian grocery stores.

BONITO FLAKES (KATSUOBOSHI)
Katsuobushi is dried and fermented bonito. It is available from Asian grocers in the form of shaved, thin flakes. We use bonito flakes to make dashi, soups and our sesame ginger sauce. It has lots of umami. You can also make onigiri (rice balls) with it, use it as furikake (rice seasoning), or serve it with fresh tofu and okonomi-yaki (Japanese pancake).

DAIKON (WHITE RADISH)
If you want to add a touch of Japanese flavour to your dishes, daikon is the perfect vegetable. It is a staple in Japanese cooking — raw in salads; cooked in various dishes and soups; made into pickles; as a sauce, and grated as a garnish. It is traditionally a winter vegetable, but you can buy it all year round. It goes well with all kinds of Japanese sauces, such as miso, soy, vinegar, sesame and yuzu.

DASHI (STOCK)
The most important flavour in Japanese cooking — it is said that good cooking depends on the quality of the dashi. A lot of authentic Japanese cuisine is cooked with dashi as the core flavouring with salt, sugar, soy sauce and other ingredients. The three basic dashis in Japanese cooking are kombu dashi; kombu and bonito dashi; and niboshi dashi (made with small dried sardines). At CIBI, the dashi we use for our miso soup is made with kombu and bonito flakes.

GINGER
One of the key spices in Japanese cooking, fresh ginger is often grated and mixed with soy sauce for marinating or sliced in thin sticks as a garnish. It is used as a bouquet garni in Japanese and Chinese cooking, while pickled ginger is a well-known side dish with sushi. Ginger is also great for baked sweets and can be turned into syrup for tea. Ginger adds a distinct, fresh flavour and is great for your health.

GREEN TEA (MATCHA) POWDER

Matcha is a finely ground tea made from ten-cha. Its cultivation and processing is very similar to gyokuro (high-quality green tea), which is primarily used in Japanese tea ceremonies. Matcha is also a popular flavour for ice cream and other sweets. Matcha powder is sold in small containers at Japanese or large Asian grocers.

JAPANESE BEAN CURD

Japanese bean curd is light and thin — similar to the Chinese puffy bean curd, but bigger. We use it in salads or soups or pan-fry it. It is also cooked in soy and mirin with other vegetables and used as the pouch in inari sushi. You can buy it at Japanese grocers, or substitute it with puffy Chinese bean curd from Asian grocers.

HIJIKI SEAWEED, DRIED

High in minerals, this seaweed variety has fine, dark pieces that look like black long-grain rice. Hijiki is always sold dry, so you need to rehydrate it before cooking. It readily absorbs liquid, so it is usually cooked in soy sauce and sugar to give it more flavour, then tossed with other vegetables.

JAPANESE MAYONNAISE

Japanese mayonnaise tastes different than other types of mayonnaise. It is usually made with egg yolk, rice vinegar and vegetable oils such as canola or soybean, so the flavour is light and the texture is thick. We sometimes use mayonnaise as a dressing, mixing it with other spices and herbs. When you make potato salad, this is the perfect mayonnaise to use.

JAPANESE MUSTARD (KARASHI)

Japanese mustard is hot and strong and is available as a paste or in powder form. You can use hot English mustard as a substitute.

JAPANESE SEVEN SPICE (SHICHIMI-TOGARASHI)

A blend of spices based on togarashi (chilli), it adds pep when sprinkled on top of noodle dishes such as ramen, soba and udon as well as hot pots, soups, yaki-tori and donburi dishes. At CIBI, we make our own shichimi blend using fresh chilli, roasted chilli, dried yuzu peel, sansho pepper, white poppy seeds and toasted black sesame seeds.

KOJI

Koji is a fungus culture used for fermentation and has been part of Japanese cuisine for centuries. It is typically used in making sake, miso, vinegar, soy sauce and pickles. We use koji as a dressing, blending it with natto (fermented soybeans), to marinate meat and pickle vegetables. Marinating meat with koji makes it very tender and gives a great umami taste. Rice koji is the most commonly available form. You will find it sold as blocks at Japanese grocers.

KOMBU (DRIED KELP)

A dark green seaweed that's often dried in large leaves. We use kombu for stock or to pickle vegetables. At home, I use kombu for dashi, in a hot pot or to make vegetable soup — it has so much umami. Once you have it in your pantry, it becomes very handy for cooking a wide variety of Japanese dishes. When boiled, kombu swells as it rehydrates. It can then be chopped up and added to salads and other dishes. It is very nutritious and has lots of minerals.

MIRIN

Mirin is a type of rice wine, lower in alcohol and higher in sugar content than sake. My mother-in-law often uses mirin in her cooking. She says that a little touch of mirin makes a dish soft and round, richer and deeper, and I agree with her. Japanese cooking uses quite a lot of sugar, but I try to use mirin instead of sugar where I can.

MISO

A traditional Japanese seasoning made by fermenting rice, barley and/or soybeans with salt and kojikin (yeast). The most common miso is made with soybeans. The result is a thick paste used for sauces and spreads, pickling vegetables or meats and mixing with dashi to make miso soup. High in protein and rich in vitamins and minerals, miso is typically salty. Its flavour and aroma depend on various factors, including the blend of ingredients and the fermentation process used.

MIZUNA

We use mizuna leaves quite a lot in the CIBI kitchen. Using mizuna in a salad gives it a very Japanese look; just mix it with other salad ingredients and one of our Japanese-inspired dressings for a simple, beautiful dish. If you can't get mizuna, other salad leaves such as iceberg or cos (romaine) lettuce make a good substitute.

OLIVE OIL

We use olive oil in our cooking, and extra-virgin olive oil for dressings and sauces. Using good quality extra-virgin olive oil is very important to make your sauces and dressings tasty and satisfying — a good oil makes even the simplest avocado dish very special. Our extra-virgin olive oil is from McLaren Vale in South Australia and we love it.

RENKON (LOTUS ROOT)

Lotus root is a versatile vegetable, and can be used for pickling, frying and braising. At CIBI, we make renkon stuffed with tofu, renkon chips, su-renkon (pickled renkon) and grated renkon cake. Often used in Oshou-gatsu (New Year) dishes, it is said that you can see the future through its holes. You can buy fresh renkon or frozen renkon slices at a Japanese or Asian grocery store. Fresh renkon starts changing colour as soon as it is cut, so always soak it in vinegar and water before cooking to stop it from discolouring.

RICE, BROWN AND WHITE

For white rice, I use a medium-grain variety — usually koshihikari or akitakomachi, which you can find at Japanese grocers. At CIBI, we use medium-grain brown rice. Eating brown rice alone is sometimes a little bit heavy, so I recommend blending it with white rice — it creates a perfect balance of flavour and nutrition. At home, I serve brown rice with olive oil, kombu and a bit of salt, and it tastes amazing.

RICE VINEGAR

This vinegar pairs well with the umami and sweetness of rice, making it perfect for sushi rice. Grain vinegars are commonly used in Japanese cooking. They are great for pickling, making dressings and marinating. I recommend using rice vinegar in all your Japanese recipes, and, for a subtle, tasty twist, you can substitute wine or sherry vinegar with rice vinegar in other dishes, too.

SAKE/COOKING SAKE

Sake is a Japanese rice wine made by fermenting rice with koji and water. We use cooking sake in our kitchen, available at Japanese or Asian grocers. It adds richness and umami, and it also reduces the odours of fish and meat. If you cannot find cooking sake, you can use drinking sake.

SESAME OIL

Made from toasted white sesame seeds, sesame oil has a brown-golden colour with dense aromas. It is used for tempura, deep-frying, stir-fries, or drizzled as a finishing touch. It is available from Asian grocers or supermarkets.

SESAME SEEDS, TOASTED

We use toasted white and black sesame seeds a lot in our recipes and dressings, and often grind them on top of salads or other dishes. With their anti-aging properties, sesame seeds are great for your health. Look for ready-toasted sesame seeds at Japanese or Asian grocers, or make your own by toasting them over a low heat for a few minutes.

SHIITAKE MUSHROOMS

My parents grow shiitake in the mountains close to home. I use them in soup, and they also add richness and depth when making dashi. If you can't get fresh shiitake mushrooms, you can buy dried shiitake from Asian grocers or large supermarkets.

SHISO LEAVES

We love shiso, which is a fragrant, flavoursome Japanese basil. There are two types of shiso leaves: red and green. In summer, there is always heaps of shiso growing in my grandma's vegetable garden, and she uses red shiso leaves to preserve umeboshi (Japanese sour plums). Shiso is wonderful used fresh in salads, tempura, sauces and many dressings.

SOBA NOODLES

Soba is Japanese for 'buckwheat' and is one of the best-known Japanese noodles. They have less calories than other noodles and pastas and are high in fibre and vitamins. Pure buckwheat is wheat-free, but buckwheat noodles are generally made with both buckwheat and wheat flour. Soba noodles are traditionally served either chilled with a dipping sauce or in hot broth. At CIBI, we make salads with soba noodles.

SOYBEANS

Along with azuki beans, soybeans are probably the most common hard beans you'll find in Japanese cooking. We often cook soybeans with rice. Adding them to rice turns a simple bowl into a tasty and nutritious dish. You can get soybeans from organic or Asian grocers. Soak them in water a day before you cook them.

SOY SAUCE

We grew up with soy sauce — there was always a bottle on the dining table. While it isn't in every Japanese dish, you can't talk about Japanese cuisine without it! In the CIBI kitchen, we use soy sauce in many ways: for dressing, marinating, braising, in soup and for pickling.

SPRING ONION (SCALLIONS)

An iconic Asian garnish. We finely chop our spring onion and sprinkle it over the top of a dish at the very last moment. Spring onion and ginger are our version of a bouquet garni when making Japanese chicken stock or slow-cooked cha-shu pork.

TAHINI, UNHULLED

Unhulled tahini has a darker colour and stronger, richer flavour than hulled tahini, making it a better match for Japanese cooking. I've found unhulled tahini is very close to Japanese white sesame paste. You can usually find it at a health food or organic shop. We use it for making sesame dressing, fish and meat dishes. It's also great in baked goods and with ice cream or panna cotta.

TAMARI

Tamari is a soy sauce made exclusively from soybeans, while most soy sauce is made from soybeans and wheat. Tamari is darker in colour, has more umami, and its flavour is richer and stronger. In Australia, tamari is commonly used as a gluten-free soy sauce alternative. In Japan, it is commonly used for dipping sashimi or making teriyaki sauce.

TOFU

These days you can buy many kinds of tofu, often combined with different ingredients and flavours. In our recipes we use plain tofu, which comes in two forms — silken and momen (firm). Silken is light, smooth and very soft. On the other hand, momen is harder and more dense. We use silken for salads or soups and momen for our tofu patties.

UMEBOSHI (JAPANESE SOUR PLUMS)

This is an iconic Japanese pickle. My grandma would brine ume during the rainy season in Japan, then dry them in the sun at the beginning of summer before pickling them with red shiso leaves. Umeboshi are very sour and salty, served as a side dish with rice or eaten with onigiri (rice balls) for breakfast and lunch. We also make umeboshi dressing for salad and sashimi.

WAKAME SEAWEED

Wakame is most commonly sold in dried form, although it is also available in salted form. Wakame is high in minerals and has a subtle sweet flavour. We often use wakame in summery salads and wintery soups. Soak dried wakame in water for about 5 minutes to rehydrate it before using.

WHITE SOY SAUCE

White soy sauce is a light amber-coloured soy sauce often used in Kyoto to make dashi or dipping sauce. It's a little bit fancy: even in Japan, you need to go to a special grocery store to get it. It has a subtler flavour than soy sauce, which preserves the flavour of dashi, and it's great when you want to make sauce or soup that is lighter in colour.

YUZU JUICE

Yuzu is a Japanese winter citrus, roughly the size and shape of a mandarin. It is strong, fragrant and tastes like something between a lemon and a grapefruit, and is used in similar ways. Yuzu zest is served in soups or as a garnish. Yuzu jam is also quite common in Japan. On its own, the juice is great for dressings — it's very tangy, with beautiful aromas. We use yuzu juice in drinks at CIBI and to make our yuzu ponzu.

YUZU PEPPER

A fermented paste made from chilli peppers, yuzu peel and salt. You don't need much, as it is very spicy. We often use it in noodle dishes, salad dressings, with braised meat, tofu and hot pots.

SAUCES and DRESSINGS

The key to impressing with a simple dish is often the sauce or dressing you use. The sauces below are full of Japanese ingredients and will definitely make your dining experience more exciting! They are not only for Japanese dishes, either – try them with barbecued meat, roasted veggies or sandwiches – anything you like. They will add a beautiful Japanese touch and unique flavours to all of your favourite meals.

All of these sauces can be made in bulk, sealed tightly and kept in the fridge. Most will last for a good couple of months, so you don't have to make a new batch every time you want to use it.

MISO BASED

SWEET LEMON MISO SAUCE
MAKES 240 ML (8 FL OZ)

90 g (3 oz) white miso

90 ml (3 fl oz) mirin

60 g (2 oz) sugar

zest of 1 lemon

juice of 1 lemon

In a small bowl, combine the ingredients and mix well.

SWEET MISO SAUCE
MAKES 240 ML (8 FL OZ)

90 g (3 oz) white miso

90 ml (3 fl oz) mirin

60 g (2 oz) sugar

In a small bowl, combine the ingredients and mix well.

SWEET CHILLI MISO SAUCE
MAKES 250 ML (8½ FL OZ)

2 tablespoons olive oil

1 teaspoon dried chilli flakes

150 g (5½ oz) red miso

3 tablespoons mirin

3 tablespoons sugar

2 tablespoons sake

To make the chilli oil, heat the oil in a small frying pan over a medium–high heat. Once the oil is hot, add the chilli flakes. Stir well for a couple of minutes to infuse the chilli, then turn off the heat. In a small bowl, combine all of the ingredients and mix well.

KARASHI MISO SAUCE
MAKES 200 ML (7 FL OZ)

1 tablespoon karashi powder	2 tablespoons rice vinegar
80 g (2¾ oz) white miso	2 tablespoons sugar
2 tablespoons mirin	1½ tablespoons sake

To make the karashi paste, mix 2 tablespoons water and the karashi powder in a bowl. Add the rest of the ingredients and mix well. If you can get a tube of pre-made karashi paste at a Japanese grocer, you can use that instead.

BARBECUE MISO SAUCE
MAKES 200 ML (7 FL OZ)

60 g (2 oz/¼ cup) red miso	½ red apple, cored and chopped into small pieces
60 ml (2 fl oz/¼ cup) mirin	3 cm (1¼ in) piece of fresh ginger, grated
2 tablespoons sake	
2 tablespoons honey	1 small garlic clove, finely chopped
1 tablespoon soy sauce	½ small red chilli

Put all of the ingredients in a blender and blend into a nice, smooth paste.

GINGER MISO SAUCE

Though none of my recipes in this book call for this sauce, it is so good that I wanted to share it! This is great with blanched or cooked greens, or even with plain rice.

MAKES 150 ML (5 FL OZ)

6–7 cm (2½–2¾ in) piece of fresh ginger, grated

60 g (2 oz/ ¼ cup) red miso

2 tablespoons mirin

2 tablespoons sugar

In a small bowl, combine the ingredients and mix well.

SOY and SESAME SEED BASED

SOY VINAIGRETTE
MAKES 200 ML (7 FL OZ)

70 ml (2¼ fl oz) soy sauce

100 ml (3½ fl oz) rice vinegar

2 tablespoons sesame oil

In a small bowl, combine the ingredients and mix well.

NANBAN SAUCE
MAKES 180 ML (6 FL OZ)

90 ml (3 fl oz) rice vinegar

60 ml (2 fl oz/ ¼ cup) soy sauce

2 tablespoons mirin

In a small bowl, combine the ingredients and mix well.

GOMA-DARE (SESAME DRESSING)
MAKES 220 ML (7½ FL OZ)

50 g (1¾ oz) toasted white sesame seeds

2 tablespoons sugar

2 tablespoons tamari

1½ tablespoons mirin

1¼ tablespoons sesame oil

1 tablespoon sake

1 tablespoon rice vinegar

2 tablespoons unhulled tahini

Put the sesame seeds in a small blender and blend until crushed. Add the other ingredients and 1⅔ tablespoons water and blend well.

SESAME GINGER
MAKES 190 G (6½ OZ)

3–4 cm (1¼ –1½ in) piece of fresh ginger, grated

1 handful bonito flakes

100 g (3½ oz) toasted white sesame seeds

1 tablespoon mirin

60 ml (2 fl oz/¼ cup) tamari or soy sauce

Add the sesame seeds to a small blender and blend until crushed. In a small bowl, combine the ingredients and mix well.

SESAME SAUCE
MAKES 180 ML (6 FL OZ)

60 g (2 oz/¼ cup) unhulled tahini

2 tablespoons sesame oil

2 tablespoons sugar

2 tablespoons tamari

2 teaspoons rice vinegar

In a bowl, combine the ingredients with 2 tablespoons water and whisk well.

YUZU PONZU
MAKES 180 ML (6 FL OZ)

90 ml (3 fl oz) soy sauce

3 tablespoons rice vinegar

3 tablespoons yuzu juice (or lemon, if you can't find yuzu)

In a small bowl, combine the ingredients and mix well.

VINEGAR BASED

UME (PLUM) DRESSING
MAKES 180 ML (6 FL OZ)

100 ml (3½ fl oz) rice vinegar

3 tablespoons extra-virgin olive oil

1½ tablespoons sour plum flesh (about 3 sour plums), finely chopped

1 tablespoon sugar

½ teaspoon salt

Combine all of the ingredients in a lidded jar and shake well.

TAHINI GINGER DRESSING
MAKES 180 ML (6 FL OZ)

3 cm (1¼ in) piece of fresh ginger, grated

60 g (2 oz) Lebanese tahini

60 ml (2 fl oz/ ¼ cup) mirin

3 tablespoons rice vinegar

½ teaspoon sugar

¼ teaspoon tamari

¼ teaspoon salt

Combine all of the ingredients and 1 tablespoon water in a lidded jar and shake well.

AMAZU
MAKES 260 ML (9 FL OZ)

200 ml (7 fl oz) rice vinegar

40 g (1½ oz) sugar

½ teaspoon salt

In a small bowl, combine the ingredients and mix well.

HONEY MUSTARD DRESSING
MAKES 180 ML (6 FL OZ)

90 ml (3 fl oz) extra-virgin olive oil

60 ml (2 fl oz/ ¼ cup) lemon juice

2 tablespoons honey

⅔ tablespoon seeded mustard

Combine all of the ingredients in a lidded jar and shake well.

YUZU PEPPER DRESSING
MAKES 165 ML (5½ FL OZ)

90 ml (3 fl oz) extra-virgin olive oil

3 tablespoons rice vinegar

1½ teaspoons yuzu pepper paste

3 teaspoons sugar

Combine all of the ingredients in a lidded jar and shake well.

YUZU PEPPER MAYO DRESSING
MAKES 195 ML (6½ FL OZ)

90 ml (3 fl oz) rice vinegar

3 tablespoons extra-virgin olive oil

3 tablespoons Japanese mayonnaise

3 teaspoons sugar

¼ teaspoon salt

¾ teaspoon yuzu pepper

Combine all of the ingredients in a lidded jar and shake well.

ESSENTIAL KITCHEN TOOLS

We would like to share with you our secret loves in the kitchen – tools designed to simplify the preparation of Japanese (and many other) dishes. It is no surprise that, with its rich heritage, Japanese cuisine has produced a range of kitchen tools to perfectly fit the tasks required (from cutting and cleaning to preparing ingredients such as miso and ginger), and that blend simplicity and functionality with natural materials to ensure they last a long time. A delight to handle, they're sure to become essentials in your kitchen.

AKUTORI STRAINER
This skimmer ladle made from a fine wire mesh is used for removing unwanted bits of food or skimming the foam from the surface of liquids while cooking. It comes in handy for picking up random bits of batter in the oil while making tempura or kara-age (deep-fried chicken), or skimming the foam off soup.

CABBAGE SLICER
If you are thinking of making tonkatsu (Japanese pork schnitzel) for dinner, a cabbage slicer is a must-have for shredding the cabbage that will be served on the side. Cabbage slicers are a bit wider than regular vegetable slicers, they fit about a quarter of a cabbage. They are also great for slicing hard vegetables like carrots, daikon and cucumber. It's a handy tool that we use every day in the CIBI kitchen.

CAST-IRON POTS AND PANS (NANBU-TEKKI)
Cast-iron pots and pans are pleasing to the eye and make our food look even better – they can be taken right from the oven to the table. So functional and beautiful, and they last forever. Their simple design, durable material and superb utility are why we love having them on our cooktop and dining table.

COPPER GRATER
We all need a good grater. Copper graters not only look stylish, but also bring pleasure to the task of grating garlic, ginger, lemon and daikon – with a copper grater, you can grate vegetables very finely. When you wash your hands after grating, simply let hot water stream over the grater to clean it. Even cleaning up is a pleasure!

ENAMEL TRAYS
These trays are both beautiful and practical: you can cook your meals and serve in them. Enamelware is long lasting, doesn't produce environmental toxins and keeps food fresh and germ-free, making it ideal for storage.

FISH BONE TWEEZERS
Fish bone tweezers make removing fish bones easy. There are quirky, fun designs available (including fish shapes), so you can use them as a table or kitchen decoration.

JAPANESE COPPER OMELETTE PAN
We use a square pan for making tamago-yaki (Japanese omelettes). It's a cooking ritual: pour your egg mix in, make an omelette, roll it up to one end of the pan, lift it up and pour more egg mix underneath it.

JAPANESE KNIVES
Japanese-steel knives add style and sharpness to the kitchen. They cut beautifully and provide the satisfaction and sensation of using a well-made tool appropriate to the task, heightening your enjoyment of each ingredient. Using it may sharpen your appetite as well! Japanese knives are designed for specific tasks, so you may want to use them individually for the different ingredients you're working with. The Deba bocho is used to cut and fillet fish. The Nakiri bocho is for cutting vegetables, and the Sashimi bocho is for thinly slicing fish for sashimi.

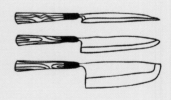

KAMENOKO TAWASHI (TURTLE BRUSH)
A tawashi is a traditional Japanese scrubbing brush made from hemp palm fibre and is used for washing off dirt and mud. It is hard and durable, yet flexible – excellent for scrubbing potatoes and other root vegetables, washing kitchen utensils, bathtubs, muddy shoes and the like. It should not be used for scrubbing delicate goods like small children, no matter how much you are tempted! After use, simply shake it out and leave it to dry.

MANAITA (WOODEN CUTTING BOARD)
Before plastic and various other compounds took over, the cutting board was made of wood. In Japan, it was made from select hardwoods that include keyaki (*Zelkova serrata*), Japanese cypress, ginkgo and magnolia, reflecting the regional availability of trees. I use a Japanese cypress board, known for its natural disinfectant properties, fresh scent, lightness and durability.

MISO KOSHI (MISO STRAINER)

This strainer is specially made for miso soup. The mesh is semi-coarse, allowing many of the flavoursome solids to pass through while keeping out larger bits of koji rice. The strainer comes with a wooden pestle used to incorporate the miso into the dashi. Press the miso against the strainer to gently add it to your soup.

OTOSHI-BUTA (DROP LID)

Otoshi-buta are Japanese-style drop lids used for simmering a range of dishes. They are often round wooden lids that float on top of simmering liquid to ensure heat is evenly distributed. It also reduces the chances of large bubbles forming, keeping fragile ingredients from being damaged. In this book, we use a circle of baking paper — also known as a cartouche — as a drop lid.

SAI-BASHI (CHEF'S CHOPSTICKS)

Once you've mastered eating with chopsticks, we recommend cooking with them. Simple and convenient, the longer, fatter sai-bashi have serrated ends for easy gripping of ingredients. They are ideal for handling food with one hand, picking food out of the pan and arranging food on the plate.

SESAME GRINDER

Sesame grinders use a rotary knob to grind sesame seeds directly onto salad, or steamed or sautéed vegetables. We recommend you use toasted sesame seeds, which you can find at Japanese or Asian grocers.

SHAMOJI (RICE SCOOP)

For beautiful cooked rice, you need a wooden scoop to serve it with. What better implement to use than something natural — a shamoji is the perfect match. Dampen the spoon before using to stop rice from sticking to it.

STAINLESS STEEL BOWLS AND STRAINERS

Great for mixing, stirring, serving, draining (but not for wearing as a helmet), quality stainless steel bowls and strainers are simple, but beautiful — tools you will cherish for a long time to come. They are carefully shaped to provide maximum practicality and functionality.

STAINLESS STEEL TONGS

Good-quality stainless steel tongs make cooking easy and satisfying. Our kids love using our Sori Yanagi tongs — give them a try and you won't be disappointed! They look fantastic and stylish, and will never spring out too far.

SOY SAUCE BOTTLE

Soy sauce is a staple seasoning in Japanese cooking, omnipresent in the kitchen and on the dining table. It is used in great quantities in the kitchen, and presented on the table so that everyone can add their own. A simple, beautiful soy sauce bottle is the ultimate expression of form and function.

SURIBACHI AND SURIKOGI (JAPANESE MORTAR AND PESTLE)

The Japanese version of the mortar and pestle is used for crushing various ingredients, most commonly sesame seeds. The suribachi is a pottery bowl, glazed on the outside and with a rough pattern called kushi-no-me that has a texture similar to an oroshigane (grater) on the inside. The surikogi is made from wood to avoid wear on the suribachi. Set the bowl on a non-slip surface, such as a damp towel, and use the surikogi to grind the ingredients.

SUSHI-OKE

Traditionally, a sushi-oke (a round, flat-bottomed wooden tub) is used to prepare su-meshi (vinegared rice). The wood absorbs extra moisture, so it keeps the rice nice and fluffy. If using a wooden tub, make sure to wet it with cold water and give it a quick wipe with a tea towel (dish towel).

TENUGUI

Tenugui is a hand-dyed rectangular cloth traditionally used in Japan for daily rituals as a towel, bandana, or handkerchief, and for gift-wrapping. This hand-dyed fabric is a handy everyday tool, and the designs will add colour to your lifestyle. It's great in the kitchen as a hand towel and for covering steaming rice. You can also use it to decorate your dining table or as napkins for your guests.

UROKOTORI (FISH SCALER)

The urokotori is used in Japanese cuisine to remove scales from a fish's skin before cooking. It's much easier than using a knife and minimises the risk of cutting the fish's skin or your hand. This scaler is built with a jagged stripping blade that lifts the scale while the curved buffer opposite the blade keeps the scales from being thrown in random directions. Made from stainless steel, it is easy to clean after each use.

OUR STORE

The products from our favourite artisan manufacturers available at the CIBI store are iconic classics that have stood the test of time, some for decades. Simple yet timeless, precious yet to be enjoyed and appreciated, they are used in millions of homes in Japan. Every time you use these well-crafted items, whether it be a cast-iron pot or fine porcelain cups, you'll appreciate their beauty, simplicity, craftsmanship and functionality anew.

Tenugui Kamawanu (Daikanyama, Tokyo)

Tenugui is a rectangular piece of hand-dyed fabric that you can use in whatever way takes your fancy. Over the centuries, tenugui has been used as a business card, to wrap things up and as a towel. Made with myriad patterns, stories, characters and styles, it can be used as a scarf, table runner, tea towel (dish towel), or decorative piece to brighten up your day. It's also a highly versatile tool with a myriad of everyday uses in and around the house, the outdoors – even camping.

Our tenugui are made by Kamawanu, the leading tenugui-maker in Japan. They believe that the different fabrics and patterns of tenugui provide a window into Japanese culture. We love how this simple fabric has become woven into cultural history as a simple tool that can be used as part of everyday life.

Sori Yanagi Design

Sori Yanagi (1915–2011) was a Japanese designer who has long been close to our hearts. Sori Yanagi kitchenware and tableware has a universal and timeless appeal. The designs are rooted in the 'folk art' simplicity of Japanese craftsmanship and are meticulously designed and manufactured to provide pleasurable functionality that will last for years.

Hakusan Porcelain
(Hasami, Nagasaki)

Hakusan Porcelain makes its home in Hasami, a small town with a population of 15,000 and a 400-year history of porcelain production. Masahiro Mori (1927–2005), one of the most well-known porcelain designers in Japan, designed many pieces of porcelain for Hakusan. His philosophy was 'the pleasure in design comes from always thinking about and creating utsuwa (tableware) for daily life, which we can share with as many people as possible'. A leading ceramics manufacturer since 1779, Hakusan's philosophy is 'simple is beautiful', and their knowledge, history and technique make them industry leaders. Their approach is to always produce practical goods for everyday use that enhance the quality of daily life. They believe beautifully designed ceramics are simple yet special.

Shotoku Glass
(Sumida, Tokyo)

Hand-blown and finished by master craftsmen at Shotoku Glass in the old Sumida district of downtown Tokyo, Usuhari glass combines ultra-thin elegance with the strength required for regular use. The thinness of Usuhari glass is a tribute to the skill of its makers, with each glass handmade by master craftsmen using the same techniques that were traditionally used for making glass lightbulbs. The feel of it in your hands, the sound ice makes when it is swirled in the glass, and the fineness of the rim are truly exquisite, and unique to this glass.

INDEX

MEG and ZENTA'S STORY

Meg was born and raised in a small town surrounded by mountains in Okayama Prefecture in Japan. Living with her great-grandmother, grandparents, parents, younger sister and brother and an old black cat in a house surrounded by vegetable and rice fields, she grew up in an environment where she was tuned into food, developed her palate and intuitively knew what eating good food was all about. Most nights, her grandmother would cook traditional Japanese dishes, and when her mum came home from work she would complement them with east-meets-west-style mains. Meg still remembers being excited about going to restaurants with her foodie dad, and the time she ate buri-no-aradaki (off-cuts of yellowtail braised in soy and mirin) and being blown away by the taste, even as a little kid.

Growing up in the Japanese countryside, life was in rhythm with nature. Meg's family grew their own vegetables and rice, living and feeling the passing seasons. In spring, there were mountain vegetables; in summer, amazing local fruits; in autumn, mushrooms and nuts; in winter, preserved food and pickled dishes. Then there was the local seafood and fish from her aunt, who married into a family that lived by the sea. Every time they had a good catch, they would drop some off at Meg's home or they would go and eat at their aunt's place. When Meg's family picked more mountain vegetables or grew more veggies than they could eat, they gave them away or exchanged them. This support system was ingrained in their lifestyle, passed down through the generations.

Zenta grew up living in Texas, Japan, Australia and Germany. As grounded as he was in Japanese culture, his experiences with different cultures, cuisines and ways of enjoying life informed what would become the CIBI concept.

After high school, Meg moved to Osaka to study, where she experienced Osaka's regional food, warmth and entertainment. She moved to Adelaide to study wine in the 1990s, where she met Zenta, who was studying architecture. They often went to cafes, beaches, restaurants, wineries, pubs and shops together, taking in the joys of life in Australia. They moved back to Tokyo, then in 2004 they married and embarked on a four-month honeymoon in Europe. This experience of different cultures, people, lifestyles, products and buildings influenced how they see the world.

Looking to shape a new life for themselves, they settled in Melbourne. They were living behind a friend's shop in what was a converted garage when Zenta presented Meg with the idea of opening a shop and cafe – a space where people could come and enjoy a moment in life, be inspired, feel something special they could take home and talk about. A place where the food was healthy and well-balanced, underpinned by their Japanese heritage. They opened that space in Melbourne's Collingwood neighbourhood in 2008, and they called it CIBI.

In 2012 they opened a second venue, cafe Minanoie ('everyone's home'), further exploring opportunities to create balanced menus, show how simple beautiful dishes can be to make and enjoy, and to enrich their neighbourhood through collaborations and special events. And in 2017, they opened CIBI in Tokyo in a shitamachi (old downtown) neighbourhood, introducing their philosophy of 'head, hands, heart' (and an Australian twist) to the country that first inspired them to embark on their CIBI adventure.

ARIGATO

What an amazing journey! When we started CIBI, I had a personal goal of creating food that would be worthy of a CIBI cookbook in 10 years' time. And exactly 10 years later, our book is ready! We enjoyed every moment of making this book with amazing people who supported us all the way through the process of getting it where it is now – in your hands.

To our dear friend, Mark Campbell: if we didn't see you at Minanoie at the end of 2016, this book may never have happened. Thank you for your vital energy and encouragement of who we are and what we do. We've appreciated your friendship ever since we met at CIBI.

Jane Willson, we can't thank you enough for bringing us all this way. With your energy and care, we loved the journey so much. Trisha, designer and dear friend, what a beautiful lady you are. We can't thank you enough for supporting us gently, but with great focus, and for keeping the concept and its design strong. To our wonderful publishing team, Anna Collett, Mark Roper and Kate Armstrong: thank you heaps for your great energy and beautiful work, and the care that enabled this book to become reality. Leo Greenfield and Morgan Hickinbotham, thank you for being our CIBI family for many years. We are grateful that your beautiful work has become part of this book.

Dion Lenting, one of our dearest friends in Japan, has been helping us with writing since we opened CIBI in 2008. Without you, we couldn't have made the book as perfect as it is. Thank you for being our very good friend and a part of the CIBI family.

And Nana: what an amazing person you are. You are a big part of our family. Thank you for your hardworking, endless efforts and your love of CIBI.

To our team in Melbourne and Tokyo, we are so lucky to have you in our family – we appreciate your work and energy in bringing the CIBI experience to life. To our customers and CIBI fans and friends who have been supporting us since we opened the door in 2008: you know who we are talking about. We love having you every day, every week and month coming and bringing our space to life. Thank you!

To our manufacturers in Japan: without you, our book would not be as beautiful as it is! Your passion for design and functionality, and commitment to artisan production, has been a source of inspiration. We are so happy to share your work with a wider world.

To the suppliers who provide the vegetables, seafood, meat, bread and many other ingredients that make CIBI possible: thank you for your support and for bringing your smile to the store every day.

Thank you to Zenta's parents. I have learnt many things from his mum's cooking and her table decorations, and from his dad, an amazing businessperson who answers every question we ask.

To my family, neighbours and relatives in Okayama. The longer I live in Australia, the more I really thank you for everything I experienced in my childhood. Without my heritage, CIBI and this book would never have turned out this way. Thank you all for giving me this opportunity and endless support.

Finally, to our dearest family, Uta, Haru and Shun: we love you so much. You guys constantly make us think and grow as people. We look forward to watching you grow.

Meg and Zenta Tanaka

Published in 2018 by Hardie Grant Books,
an imprint of Hardie Grant Publishing

Hardie Grant Books (Melbourne)
Building 1, 658 Church Street
Richmond, Victoria 3121

Hardie Grant Books (London)
5th & 6th Floors
52–54 Southwark Street
London SE1 1UN

hardiegrantbooks.com

A Cataloguing-in-Publication entry is available
from the catalogue of the National Library of
Australia at www.nla.gov.au

CIBI. Simple Japanese-inspired meals to share
with family and friends
ISBN 978 1 74379 373 2

Publishing Director: Jane Willson
Managing Editor: Marg Bowman
Project Editor: Anna Collett
Editor: Kate J. Armstrong
Design Manager: Jessica Lowe
Designer: Trisha Garner
Photographer: Mark Roper
Stylists: Meg and Zenta Tanaka
Home Economist: Nana Hurst
Production Manager: Todd Rechner

Colour reproduction by Splitting Image Colour Studio
Printed in China by 1010 Printing International Limited